100 READINGS FOR TROUBLED TIMES

GOD IS
IN CONTROL

DEVOTIONS FOR MEN

100 READINGS FOR TROUBLED TIMES

GOD IS
IN CONTROL
DEVOTIONS FOR MEN

GLENN HASCALL

BARBOUR
PUBLISHING

Cover Design: Greg Jackson, Thinkpen Design

Published by Barbour Publishing, Inc., 1810 Barbour Drive, Uhrichsville, Ohio 44683, www.barbourbooks.com

Our mission is to inspire the world with the life-changing message of the Bible.

Member of the
Evangelical Christian
Publishers Association

Printed in China.

INTRODUCTION

Does the craziness of modern society bother you? Does consuming the news, skimming social media, and talking with everyday people leave you frustrated, depressed, even despairing? You can be sure we've all been there at one time or another.

You can also be sure that these feelings are nothing new. When you read God's Word, you'll encounter biblical characters who faced many of the same issues. Thousands of years ago, they had personal struggles, family conflicts, corrupt political leaders, serious health concerns, and the terrorizing threats of enemies.

And yet scripture keeps driving home one consistent truth: *God is in control.* He's aware of every circumstance, even humanity's worst crises (many of which we've brought onto ourselves), and He's working through them for good.

The famed nineteenth-century British preacher Charles Spurgeon highlighted a somewhat obscure scripture that pulls the curtain back to expose God's behind-the-scenes work. When the nation of Israel divided into two rival sections due to the foolish arrogance of Solomon's son Rehoboam, the new king wanted his army to invade and punish the seceding north. But God told His prophet,

"Speak to Rehoboam the son of Solomon, king of Judah, and to all the house of Judah and Benjamin, and to the

remnant of the people, saying, 'This is what the LORD says: "You shall not go up or fight against your brothers, the children of Israel. Return, every man to his house, for this thing is from Me."'"
1 KINGS 12:23–24 SKJV

It was Rehoboam's cocky, rude answer to the people's request for leniency that had created the national split—but God declared, "This thing is from Me." In response to this passage, Spurgeon said, "I believe in the free agency of men, in their responsibility and wickedness, and that everything evil comes of them, but I also believe in God, that 'this thing' which, on the one side of it, was purely and alone from men, on another side of it was still from God who rules both evil and good, and not only walks the garden of Eden in the cool of a summer's eve, but walks the billows of the tempestuous sea, and rules everywhere by His sovereign might."

When you look for them, you'll find dozens of biblical cases in which God was indeed working His will through people's difficult circumstances. The one hundred devotions in this book will help you see the unseen—the hand of God in every detail of life—and encourage you with the truth of His knowledge and power.

Never forget what the apostle Paul taught—that for those who love God, "we know that all things work together for good" (Romans 8:28 SKJV). That's true because *God* is the one who's working.

DECLINE THE ONE TREE

God warned [Adam], "You may freely eat the fruit of every
tree in the garden—except the tree of the knowledge of
good and evil. If you eat its fruit, you are sure to die."
GENESIS 2:16–17 NLT

The world was new. The air and water were pure. God had recently created Adam, the first man, and watched as he named all the animals. God had given him only one easy rule: avoid that one tree in the garden. To be clear—there were plenty of other trees, each of them bearing fruit. Therefore, Adam had no compelling reason to eat *that* fruit.

But wherever something is forbidden, temptation is rarely far behind.

Adam and his wife, Eve, could have said no, but their curiosity about what they couldn't have overpowered their belief in what God had said. They questioned Him and decided His singular law was not worth following.

This event was the turning point for every human in history. Because one rule was broken, every individual who would ever be born would inherit this lawbreaking attitude. And the consequence for this sin has remained the same: death. Not immediate death, perhaps, but certain death. Death follows sin. It always has.

Had God lost control? No. He already had a plan in place: His name was Jesus. John 1:14 says, "The Word [Jesus] became human and made his home among us. He was full of unfailing love and faithfulness. And we have seen his glory, the glory of the Father's one and only Son" (NLT). Jesus made forgiveness possible.

This was God's very first answer to the question of rebellion. You have broken His laws too. . .but He's already altered your outcome by inviting you to pass from death into spiritual life.

WHY IS IT IMPORTANT THAT WE ACCEPT GOD'S REMEDY FOR REBELLION? DOES KNOWING THAT GOD FORGIVES MAKE YOU WANT TO DRAW CLOSER TO HIM?

ANGER DEFLECTION

Then the LORD said to Cain, "Why are you angry? Why is your face downcast? If you do what is right, will you not be accepted? But if you do not do what is right, sin is crouching at your door; it desires to have you, but you must rule over it."
GENESIS 4:6–7 NIV

The world's first brothers chose separate career paths. Cain, the firstborn, was a successful farmer who became proud of what he'd accomplished. Abel managed livestock and was equally successful. But because the men's parents (Adam and Eve) had introduced lawbreaking to humanity, these boys were told to offer God a sacrifice for their sin. God's rule was that the only payment for sin was the shedding of blood; therefore, the sacrifice had to be an animal.

Both brothers knew this, but when the time for sacrifice approached, Abel brought animals and Cain brought vegetables and grain. As commodities, both were valuable; as sacrifices, only one was acceptable.

God rejected Cain's sacrifice. But when the Lord talked with him later, He didn't cut Cain off from Himself, but instead offered advice. Cain's anger, God suggested, was blocking his only path to forgiveness. Consequently, his sin was ready to overwhelm him. So how did Cain respond? By rejecting God. . .and taking out his homicidal fury on his brother.

This moment meant God would have to bend yet another bad circumstance in His direction. Shortly thereafter, God would give that first couple a new son named Seth, a man whose descendants would include Abraham, David, and, ultimately, Jesus—humanity's perfect blood sacrifice.

Sometimes, God's good outcomes are not easily seen. But every bad situation invites God's intervention. Count on that— even when you can't see any good in the picture.

WHY IS IT HARD TO WAIT FOR GOD'S GOOD OUTCOME?
WHEN SOMETHING BAD HAPPENS, HOW CAN
YOU TRAIN YOURSELF TO PREEMPTIVELY
THANK GOD FOR MAKING IT GOOD?

NOAH'S WOODEN SPECTACLE

Noah found grace in the eyes of the LORD.
GENESIS 6:8 SKJV

Every person on earth had given up on God. They all turned away, stopped their ears, and hardened their hearts. God's Word even says, "It grieved the LORD that He had made man on the earth" (Genesis 6:6 SKJV). God was fed up with humanity.

This could have been the time of a total divine reset. . .had it not been for one particular man and his family. In a rebellious world, Noah got God's attention by refusing to forsake Him. He followed God. He listened to the Lord. That's why God asked Noah to do something that made others ridicule him.

For decades, Noah worked to build an enormous boat on dry land. This boat was large enough to hold two of every kind of animal and even more birds. Think of the comments he must have received! Every detail of Noah's boat was likely mocked by the crowd. There wasn't even a body of water nearby that was big enough to make it seem practical.

Imagine following God, even when no one besides your own family encourages you in your decision. Imagine seeing the crowds come and go, jeering at your faith decade after decade. Imagine the faith you'd need to believe that in the midst of all these battles, God has already won the war.

Noah had that faith; as a result, Genesis 8:1 says that God remembered Noah. The Lord used the boat Noah built to save him, his family, and enough animals to fill the earth after the greatest flood the world would ever see. Noah's faith mattered.

This story is a valuable reminder that God is never slow—His pace is just different than you might expect. Waiting can be excruciating, but God never leaves you without help. Your waiting can and will have a good outcome. Just ask Noah.

WOULD YOU BE DISCOURAGED IF YOU WERE IN NOAH'S POSITION? HOW DOES CONSIDERING WHAT NOAH EXPERIENCED BEFORE THE FLOOD IMPACT THE WAY YOU VIEW PATIENCE?

THE GREAT WORD SCRAMBLE

Then [the people] said, "Come, let's build a great city for ourselves with a tower that reaches into the sky. This will make us famous and keep us from being scattered all over the world."
GENESIS 11:4 NLT

No one had seen anything like what the people were building on the plains of Babylonia: bricks, meticulously stacked, reaching farther and farther from the ground. This was a collective effort, requiring purpose and direction. There was just one problem, though: both the tower's purpose and the people's direction were wrong.

Perhaps remembering the enormous boat their relative, Noah, had built, the people adopted the attitude of "Go big or go home." They desired fame and glory. They craved recognition. They wanted to show they were strong—invincible. And since everyone spoke one language, their vision for this incredible tower was unmarred by confusion.

There was no room for God in this daring declaration of independence. They had a truly unstoppable plan. . .until it was stopped, that is. Nothing in their prideful hearts and minds could have prepared them for what happened next: God fractured their language.

Suddenly, basic communication became impossible. And since language barriers tend to complicate even the simplest of tasks, the people had no choice but to abandon their tower. Gradually, some people found others who shared their new language, and these people moved to locations where they could be with those who understood them.

So where was the good in this? After all, humanity was no longer unified. Mistrust of "outsiders" would begin to grow. Their tower was forgotten. But they *were* with people who could understand them, and those people could talk about what happened—and, with new words forming on their lips, they could admit to God that they were wrong for making such selfish and prideful plans.

Even today, God continues to work among people in every language group and nation.

WHY IS HUMAN FAME NOT WORTH PURSUING? WHAT BENEFITS MIGHT ARISE FROM HAVING MULTIPLE LANGUAGE GROUPS?

MOVING DAY

The LORD had said to Abram, "Go from your country, your people and your father's household to the land I will show you."
GENESIS 12:1 NIV

. . . .

Abram was seventy-five years old when God informed him that it was moving day. Abram's community was all he'd ever known—all his friends and relatives lived in this area. He knew his way around like the back of his hand. And now, God was telling him to. . .leave? Abram was simply too old to travel, and the journey ahead would be far more exhausting than he could have dreamed.

But still, Abram went.

Because Abram and his wife, Sarai, didn't have children, they took their nephew Lot with them. All the couple really knew was that God had promised a new place and that He would make a great nation from Abram's offspring. That meant a child would have to be born, which still hadn't happened when moving day arrived—and wouldn't happen for more than two additional decades.

Once the couple got to their divinely designated new address, they soon found that no crops would grow there. . .so they moved again for a while, this time to Egypt. Still, no child.

It would take several more moves for Abram to return to the land God had promised—all while Abram continued to wait for a son.

This man may have felt like a nomad, venturing from place to place, never fitting in and never feeling truly at home. He and his wife may have wondered why they couldn't have stayed among family and friends. Perhaps tears accompanied these moments of reflection.

Little did they know, however, that during these difficult years, God was scrubbing their past away so that they could embrace His future. God was making a new nation, but Abram and Sarai first needed to be separated from their old life—a process that took time. That new nation was coming, though—and eventually came—all because one man accepted God's eviction notice.

Once again, God's promise was kept.

HAS GOD'S DIRECTION FOR YOUR GOOD EVER FELT LIKE A PUNISHMENT? WHY DO YOU THINK GOD OFTEN REQUIRES US TO WAIT BEFORE WE CAN SEE THE GOOD?

COUNTING STARS

[God] brought [Abram] outside and said, "Look now
toward heaven and count the stars, if you are able
to number them." And He said to him, "So shall
your descendants be." And he believed in the Lord,
and He counted it to him for righteousness.
GENESIS 15:5–6 SKJV

Just in case Abram had forgotten that he would be a father, God arrived with a reminder. "Can you count the stars?" God said. "That's how big your future family will be."

This probably seemed surreal to Abram. He'd just conducted a rescue mission to bring his nephew Lot home. And as he and this young man returned, God wanted to remind Abram once more that this nephew wouldn't be his only family for long. Still, the waiting continued—but Abram chose to believe God was preparing him for fatherhood in his old age.

It's true that Abram and his wife, Sarai, attempted to fulfill God's promise in a way that wasn't God's plan. But this couple's impatience wouldn't prevent God from crafting a miracle. Through it all, God's Word says that Abram kept believing in the Lord—and that's what mattered.

When good seems delayed and hope seems out of reach,

remember Abram's endurance. Against impossible odds, Abram still believed that God was good. . .and so was His plan. No matter how long it took, a boy would one day call him "Father."

HOW CHALLENGING IS IT TO BELIEVE WHAT GOD SAYS, ESPECIALLY WHEN WE'RE SURROUNDED BY THOSE WHO DON'T? WHY DO WE OFTEN STRIVE TO PLACE A TIME LIMIT ON GOD'S ANSWER?

NEW LIFE CONSTRUCTION

God said to Abraham, "Regarding Sarai, your wife—her name will no longer be Sarai. From now on her name will be Sarah. And I will bless her and give you a son from her! Yes, I will bless her richly, and she will become the mother of many nations."

GENESIS 17:15–16 NLT

You might notice that in today's verse God is speaking to Abraham, not Abram. Is this a different man than the one you read about yesterday? No. Perhaps you recall how important it was for God to tear down Abram's past in order to clear the way for his future. Part of that demolition included his name. And in today's passage, God seems to suggest the same was true for his wife.

God's promise to make Abraham a great nation was no longer "someday"—it now had a due date. After this conversation, God sent one of His angels to declare to Abraham, "I will return to you about this time next year, and your wife, Sarah, will have a son!" (18:10 NLT) It was time to get the nursery ready.

Looking back, we can see the sweeping "bad-to-good" narrative unfolding at this point in history; however, it's easy to forget that this is also a deeply personal story involving one man and his family. Abraham was just like you in many ways, praying and wondering why it was taking God forever to answer. And like it was with Abraham, God's response to your request may not be a "no"; rather, provided it fits into His perfect plan, His "yes" might just be purposefully delayed.

Never stop waiting for a new life construction.

HOW MIGHT IMAGINING YOUR LIFE AS UNDER CONSTRUCTION GROW YOUR PATIENCE AS YOU WAIT FOR GOD TO ANSWER YOUR PRAYERS? WHAT SIGNIFICANCE LAY BEHIND ABRAHAM AND SARAH'S NEW NAMES?

THE HARD COMMAND

*God said [to Abraham], "Take your son,
your only son, whom you love—Isaac—and go
to the region of Moriah. Sacrifice him there as a
burnt offering on a mountain I will show you."*

Genesis 22:2 niv

Abraham lived through a lot of change, moving from place to place and longing for a home of his own. It would have been easy to just turn God down and finish out his life among family and friends. But God helped him shake off this lethargy and become something greater than he'd ever imagined. God promised a place, and Abraham found that place. God promised a son, and Abraham had that son. Now, after the hardest journey of his life so far, God had one final challenge for him—a test to see how much Abraham had really changed. Had this man really arrived at place of total faith in God?

The command was unthinkable: *"Sacrifice your son, Isaac."* But Genesis 22:3 shows how much God had worked in the life of Abraham: "Early the next morning Abraham got up and loaded his donkey. He took with him two of his servants and his son Isaac. When he had cut enough wood for the burnt offering, he set out for the place God had told him about" (niv).

We have no idea how he slept that night. The Bible doesn't give us a glimpse into his thoughts. We can't see his eyes to witness any hint of tears. We know only that he obeyed.

For Abraham, this circumstance was the worst imaginable. Yet he still held on to one truth: God had promised him a nation. And as Abraham raised the knife, the good outcome suddenly appeared. God stopped him and told him that his priorities had become clear: he loved God more than anything on earth, even his son.

As father and son traveled home that day, Abraham had much to think about the larger journey that had led him there—and the God who'd inspired it all.

HAVE YOU EVER CONCLUDED THAT GOD MIGHT BE ASKING TOO MUCH OF YOU? HOW MIGHT ABRAHAM'S RESPONSE CHALLENGE YOUR NOTIONS ABOUT OBEDIENCE?

THRESHOLD OF CHANGE

*[God said,] "I am with you and will take
care of you wherever you go."*
GENESIS 28:15 SKJV

Somewhere between Beer-sheba and Haran, Jacob, the grand-son of Abraham, found himself alone and weary. He grabbed a rock for a pillow, drifted off to sleep. . .and started dreaming a dream he'd never forget. From his place on the open ground, Jacob saw a ladder stretching from earth to God's throne, filled top to bottom with angels traveling up and down.

God Himself stood at the top, and He gave Jacob a series of four promises: "Your descendants shall be as the dust of the earth," "you shall spread abroad to the west and to the east and to the north and to the south," "in your descendants all the families of the earth shall be blessed," and "I am with you and will take care of you wherever you go" (verses 14–15 SKJV).

This was the same God who had made promises to Jacob's grandfather, Abraham. And now, this God was reassuring a new generation that He had not forgotten or altered any of His terms.

Jacob's life was marked by a laundry list of deceptions. Some he observed; others he performed. But with God's reassurance, his future choices would be driven by forgiveness, not by regret. Verses 20–21 make this impact clear: "Jacob vowed a vow, saying, 'If God will be with me and will take care of me in this way that I go, and will give me bread to eat and clothing to put on, so that I come again to my father's house in peace, then shall the LORD be my God'" (SKJV).

Sometimes, a reminder of God's promises and the love that drives His every response is exactly what we need to bring us to the threshold of change.

WHEN YOU FEEL UNLOVABLE, HOW CAN REVIEWING GOD'S PROMISES CHANGE YOUR PERSPECTIVE? HOW DOES JACOB'S STORY SHOW THAT GOD IS IN CONTROL?

AN UNEXPECTED REUNION

Jacob thought, "I will try to appease him by sending gifts ahead of me. When I see him in person, perhaps he will be friendly to me."

GENESIS 32:20 NLT

As a younger man, Jacob had convinced his twin brother, Esau, to trade his birthright for a bowl of stew. Then he'd convinced his father, Isaac, that he *was* Esau, thereby stealing the blessing Esau would have received near the end of Isaac's life. In response, Esau had threatened to murder Jacob. Now many years had passed since the two had intentionally separated.

But as Jacob was traveling with his family one day, he heard terrifying news: Esau, accompanied by four hundred men, was finally on his way to meet him. No doubt remembering his brother's fiery anger, Jacob naturally assumed the worst and sent gifts to avoid a sibling showdown.

Miraculously, though, he didn't need to. Genesis 33:4 says, "Then Esau ran to meet [Jacob] and embraced him, threw his arms around his neck, and kissed him. And they both wept" (NLT).

Jacob's bad situation was entirely his own fault—God didn't have to step in and help. Yet throughout the years, He'd been working in the lives of both men. These two had each married and carved out lives unbeknownst to each other. Gradually, Esau's anger transformed into a desire to see his brother. It had taken years to prepare this reconciliation, but God stepped in and brought both men beside "still waters."

If you've been separated from someone, allow God to take the time to work in your life and theirs. Then offer the forgiveness and love God has offered you. Reconciliation is a priceless and unexpected gift—never pass it up when you see the chance.

WHAT RELATIONSHIPS IN YOUR PAST SEEM BEYOND REPAIR TODAY? HOW CAN TIME AND FORGIVENESS POTENTIALLY RESTORE THEM?

THE OVERCOMER

Jacob was left alone, and a man wrestled with him till daybreak.
GENESIS 32:24 NIV

As Jacob nervously waited for a potential confrontation with his brother, he sent his family away to give himself time to think. And then, in what should have been a private, prayerful moment in the darkness, an event happened that would change his life forever: Jacob saw an intruder.

This encounter led to an all-night wrestling match. Jacob's hair was likely drenched with sweat and the dew of the darkened night, but neither adversary was willing to relent. In the struggle, Jacob forgot his upcoming meeting with Esau. He was unwilling to let go of his opponent for reasons he perhaps couldn't fully understand.

As the night wore on and Jacob's survival became less and less guaranteed, he discovered something unexpected. This was no ordinary wrestling match—Jacob was wrestling with God. Since it's forbidden to see God's face, God ended this object lesson just before dawn, leaving Jacob with the memory of spending time with God and working through his struggles. And then, as a parting gift, God blessed the man in a way that everyone would notice: the Lord changed Jacob's name, just like He had his grandfather's. Jacob would now be called *Israel*, signifying his status as an overcomer.

For us, wrestling with God may mean learning that His plan looks wildly different from ours. . .and allowing Him to bring our unruly wills entirely under His control. But why wouldn't we? God is in control, you know.

HAVE YOU EVER "WRESTLED WITH GOD" OVER AN OUTCOME
YOU DESPERATELY WANTED TO ACHIEVE? IF SO, HOW DID
GOD CHANGE YOU IN THIS DIVINE WRESTLING MATCH?

EMOTION EXPLOSION

*When [his brothers] saw [Joseph] afar off, even before he
came near to them, they conspired against him to slay him.*
GENESIS 37:18 SKJV

Jacob had twelve sons, and like all children, each had their
own temperament and personality. Some were leaders; others
followed. Some were hot-headed; others the voice of reason.

One day, all those temperaments and personalities were on
display at once. Their father, Jacob (Israel), had made it clear
that his son, Joseph, was hands down his favorite. Jacob gave
him gifts, and when the other brothers had to go to work with
the sheep, Joseph was allowed to stay home.

So when Joseph showed up in the countryside that day, his
brothers didn't think he'd come to help. They all assumed he
was there to spy on them and report back to their father. And
if he made some things up just to get them in trouble, there
would have been little they could do to stop him.

Except for one thing.

Jealousy changes people, causes them to act wildly out of
character, and makes them live in ways they'd never otherwise
choose. So in a fateful moment of exploding emotion, these
brothers did something they would later deeply regret: they

grabbed Joseph and sold him to slave traders. Then, in what they believed was a great cover-up, they told their dad that his favorite son had been killed by wild animals. And so the brothers moved on, their life no longer impacted by Joseph—or so they lied to themselves.

Little did these brothers know that their jealousy actually kick-started God's plan for Joseph—a plan that would eventually save their own lives. You'll read all about this (and the brothers' unexpected family reunion) in the next few days.

Joseph's circumstance seemingly couldn't have been worse, yet his story serves as a textbook example of God's ability to take our worst and turn it into His best.

**HAS JEALOUSY EVER IMPACTED YOUR DECISIONS?
HOW CAN WE RESIST JEALOUSY'S CORRUPTING INFLUENCE?**

THE FIRST FIVE WORDS

The LORD was with Joseph, so he succeeded in everything he did as he served in the home of his Egyptian master.
GENESIS 39:2 NLT

Today's verse was chosen specifically because of the first five words: "The LORD was with Joseph." God was with him when he was sold into slavery? *Yes.* When he was sold to his Egyptian master, Potiphar? *Yes.* When he was unjustly imprisoned? *Yes!*

It may sound strange, but God never left Joseph through this incredibly difficult period. No, He didn't make things immediately better for him. But through it all, God was gradually moving this young man through his horrible circumstances and toward a brighter future. . .all the while making sure Joseph knew God was with him.

Joseph could have acted out in anger. Who would blame him? His entire life had seemingly derailed. He lived through jealousy, mistreatment, and lies. But he remained a man of integrity, pursuing a path of peace, purity, and purpose.

Maybe you can identify with Joseph. When you go through difficult moments, it can be easy to think that because God comes close to those with broken hearts, this somehow means He immediately removes them from trouble. While He certainly can do that, there's something instructive about living through an unwanted trial. Hard days teach us what good days cannot.

Joseph loved God, and God took care of him—even when he was a slave, even when he was forgotten in prison, and even when his brothers traded him for a handful of coins. Why? Because God loved Joseph too.

HAVE YOU EVER STRUGGLED WITH THE IDEA THAT GOD ALLOWS SUFFERING, EVEN THOUGH HE DOESN'T CREATE IT? WHAT HAVE YOUR STRUGGLES TAUGHT YOU?

JOSEPH WEPT

*Deeply moved at the sight of his brother, Joseph
hurried out and looked for a place to weep.
He went into his private room and wept there.*
GENESIS 43:30 NIV

Joseph's brothers came to Egypt to buy grain—a valuable commodity, given that no one else had any. They'd heard of a man in Egypt who had the wisdom to store grain when it was plentiful a few years before. And now, as they stood before this food coordinator, they were surprised to learn he had a few questions for them.

They didn't recognize him as their brother Joseph. He was supposed to be either a slave in someone's home or likely dead somewhere along the way, not Egypt's second-in-command. They probably didn't want to think about Joseph very much. It made them feel ashamed.

Joseph's mind at the moment was tumultuous. His father would learn he was alive. His entire family would come to Egypt and survive the famine. The brothers would recognize that God had used their evil plans for good. Before he revealed all that, Joseph had to go away privately and weep.

Later, once the truth was out, he poignantly exclaimed

to his brothers: "Don't be afraid. Am I in the place of God? You intended to harm me, but God intended it for good to accomplish what is now being done, the saving of many lives. So then, don't be afraid. I will provide for you and your children.' And he reassured them and spoke kindly to them" (Genesis 50:19–21 NIV)

God was with Joseph, and He proved beyond a shadow of a doubt that He had always been in control. Any struggle we face is a small thing compared to God's goodness.

IF YOU WERE JOSEPH, WOULD YOU HAVE FORGIVEN YOUR BROTHERS? HOW HAS GOD AMAZED YOU IN THE WAY HE HANDLES AND RESOLVES YOUR STRUGGLES?

WAITING FOR RESCUE

[The Egyptians] set taskmasters over [the people of Israel] to afflict them with their burdens. And they built for Pharaoh treasure cities, Pithom and Raamses. But the more they afflicted them, the more they multiplied and grew.

EXODUS 1:11–12 SKJV

You may recall that a pharaoh chose a descendant of Abraham, Joseph, as second-in-command. You probably remember that God was with Joseph. And you certainly can't forget that it was this man who, with God's help, saved the lives of the Egyptians when a famine stripped the land of crops.

By the time the events of Exodus began, the aforementioned pharaoh had passed away, along with Joseph and his brothers. Egypt's new ruler looked at Joseph's descendants and saw only a very large group of people who weren't Egyptian. In other words, they were a threat to his throne. The days of kindness had passed—it was time to make things difficult for the family of Joseph, the man who had helped save his nation.

Joseph's good outcome had suddenly become very bad. Pharaoh told the midwives to kill all baby boys (though some refused), and the people who'd come to Egypt as guests found themselves toiling as slaves.

But God had an even bigger plan, one that wasn't going to happen overnight. In fact, the chosen one who'd deliver the people from Egypt hadn't been born yet, and he wouldn't be ready to lead until he was eighty. Perhaps God knew that the people, in order to long for the freedom that only He could give, would first have to know what they were rescued from. God was absolutely in control, but not everyone was ready for rescue.

HAVE MULTIPLE TRAGEDIES—BIG AND SMALL—
COMBINED TO MAKE YOU FEEL LIKE YOUR LIFE IS OUT
OF CONTROL? HOW CAN THIS STORY HELP YOU BELIEVE
GOD IS STILL PRODUCING A GOOD OUTCOME?

IMPOSSIBILITIES
UPSIDE DOWN

*When she could no longer hide him, she got a basket
made of papyrus reeds and waterproofed it with tar
and pitch. She put the baby in the basket and laid it
among the reeds along the bank of the Nile River.*

Exodus 2:3 NLT

He was one of the baby boys who would have died had the
midwives listened to Pharaoh. His parents hid him, not knowing
how they would keep their baby safe. Before long, people would
hear his crying. And if neighbors noticed, so would the guards.

Eventually, once it became obvious that hiding the boy
was no longer an option, a desperate family made a desperate
choice. . .and trusted God with the rest. They settled the boy
in a waterproof basket and placed it in the water near the bank
of the Nile River. The boy's sister watched from a distance to
see what would happen.

That's when a group of women came to the banks. . .and
with them, one of the most important women in the land:
Pharaoh's daughter. She noticed the basket and had it retrieved.
Sunlight played delicately on the basket's interior as the baby
boy stared innocently at the woman. She knew her father's

cruel command, but she could not—would not—allow it to be enforced in this case. When the boy's older sister stepped in and suggested she could find a Hebrew woman to nurse the baby, Pharaoh's daughter thought it was a good idea. Miraculously, the boy's own mother would care for him until he was old enough to live in the palace.

There was no longer any need to hide: this boy (whose name was now Moses) had the palace's protection. The baby would live.

Clearly, the impossible is just another tool in God's inventory. And it's in places of hopeless desperation that His invitation to trust Him rings out the loudest.

HAVE YOU EVER THOUGHT ABOUT GIVING UP IN RESPONSE TO AN OVERWHELMING TROUBLE? IN THESE DESPERATE MOMENTS, WHY IS GOD ALWAYS OUR BEST CHOICE?

LISTENING AND CONCERNED

The LORD said, "I have indeed seen the misery of my people in Egypt. I have heard them crying out because of their slave drivers, and I am concerned about their suffering. So I have come down to rescue them."

EXODUS 3:7–8 NIV

The people of Israel, who probably numbered nearly a million by now, had seen cruelty beyond words while living in Egypt. No longer considered guests, these once-free men and women lived as slaves for the new Pharaoh. They worked in impossible conditions with minimal supplies and a tight deadline. Now they were doing the only rational thing they could—crying out to God for help.

How did God respond? Did He kindly comment that they were in His thoughts? Did He blame them for their suffering? Did He just encourage them by saying that at some point, the Egyptians would cool their oppression? No. Instead, He gave three statements that provided immediate encouragement: God had "seen the misery of the people," He had "heard them crying out because of their slave drivers," and He was "concerned about their suffering." But His fourth declaration was truly their salvation: He promised to "come down to rescue them."

God was in charge when the Israelites came to Egypt to save their lives, and He would be in charge when they left. His deliverer was almost ready. Help was on the way.

When life becomes too much for you to handle, that's a good time to remember the God who sees, hears, shows His concern, and jumps at the chance to help.

WHAT'S YOUR KNEE—JERK REACTION TO UNWANTED
CIRCUMSTANCES? DOES IT SEEM EASIER TO
TRY FIGURING THINGS OUT YOURSELF BEFORE
ASKING GOD FOR HELP? IF SO, WHY?

REINVENTED

Moses answered and said, "But, behold, they will not believe me or listen to my voice. For they will say, 'The LORD has not appeared to you.'"
EXODUS 4:1 SKJV

Life hadn't worked out quite the way Moses had hoped. He'd been rescued from death as an infant, raised in Pharaoh's palace, and eventually driven by fear into the wilderness. Now, he spent his days raising livestock there with his wife and sons. He had no close friends or social life. It seemed his best days were behind him.

Until the day God spoke to him, giving him a task that seemed more befitting for a superhero than for a humble livestock manager. God told Moses to rescue his own suffering people.

Surely there must've been a mistake. Wouldn't God want someone younger and stronger, someone who had a more personal stake in the matter? But this wasn't an interview—it was a job assignment. Moses' excuses couldn't change the fact that God's rescue was already set in stone. All Moses had to do was show up and follow God's orders. Moses needed courage; the people needed freedom. So God provided both.

When we see big needs, it's easy to push the problem onto

"other people"—those with more money or prestige. But sometimes God's plan doesn't involve "other people"—He's chosen *you* to help turn someone's bad situation into good. All you need to do is believe. . .and just obey.

HOW DOES MOSES' "SHEPHERD-TO-DELIVERER" STORY GIVE YOU COURAGE TO FACE YOUR OWN FORMIDABLE PROBLEMS? CAN YOU THINK OF AN AREA WHERE YOU NEED TO TRUST GOD MORE?

PURSUIT OF FREEDOM

*[God said,] "I am the LORD. I will free you from your oppression
and will rescue you from your slavery in Egypt. I will redeem
you with a powerful arm and great acts of judgment."*
EXODUS 6:6 NLT

The people had cried out to God, begging for relief. And God
had listened. He chose Moses to be their deliverer. . .but before
he went to Egypt, God gave him a crash course on faith. The
Lord told Moses what he needed to do and even offered him
the help of his brother, Aaron.

It wouldn't be easy. Pharaoh saw the people as a workforce
and nothing more, so it would take far more than a polite
request to convince him to relinquish his grip. And through it
all, the Israelites themselves would accuse Moses of just making
things worse.

Both the Israelites and the Egyptians, however, would soon
learn that God is bigger than the demand of a pharaoh and wiser
than any human strategy. They'd watch as God, in the face of
impossible odds, supplied Israel's needs, protected them from
enemies, and taught them what it feels like to be free. That last
part would take the longest.

Once again, God was about to take an abysmal situation

and make it wonderful.

You were made to pursue freedom. There are a host of slavedrivers in the world. . .and sometimes, they aren't even people. Narcotics, gambling, tobacco, sex, or even food—all can enslave. You can find freedom, however, by trusting God and staying alert to the guides and helpers He sends.

Seek freedom—it's available now.

WHY DOES GOD CARE THAT YOU EXPERIENCE HIS DEFINITION OF FREEDOM? HOW HAS THIS TYPE OF FREEDOM ALTERED YOUR LIFE'S DIRECTION?

ALL OF HIM

"Didn't we say to you in Egypt, 'Leave us alone;
let us serve the Egyptians'? It would have been better for
us to serve the Egyptians than to die in the desert!"

EXODUS 14:12 NIV

It seems old habits really do die hard. Once the people of Israel left Egypt, they immediately did the one thing they'd grown accustomed to doing: they complained. Maybe they were expecting room service on their wilderness journey. But this was no glamping expedition. It was a forty-year exercise in cutting away wrong attitudes.

They often seemed to conclude that they had only two options: slavery or death. They apparently failed to realize that the God who'd brought them out of Egypt was the God who was bringing them to their new home. Think of how disappointed God must have felt! He'd saved them from slavery, only to watch them conclude that they liked slavery better after all. However, when they became too fearful to take the promised land, God continued to work with them, redirecting them into a long-term class on faith. Eventually, they'd end up exactly where God wanted them to be.

The Israelites' journey from slavery to freedom might parallel your own. You might marvel at how amazing God is one moment. . .then glamorize your old life the next. But gradually, you learn—like the Israelites did—that a little bit of God is never enough. Just as God accepts all of you, you need all of Him.

And once you understand this, new-life instruction begins.

HAVE YOU EVER THOUGHT YOU WERE BETTER OFF NOT KNOWING GOD? HOW CAN YOU REFUTE THAT CONCLUSION?

A CURSE TURNED BLESSING

Balak's anger was kindled against Balaam, and he
struck his hands together. And Balak said to Balaam,
"I called you to curse my enemies, and behold,
you have altogether blessed them these three times."
NUMBERS 24:10 SKJV

Balak did not like the people of Israel. He wanted to see them destroyed. He'd heard of a "holy" man, Balaam, who might be willing to curse the people, and Balak was willing to pay to see him do it. So in what might be history's most unique freelance gig, Balaam accepted Balak's proposition to curse for cash. However, each time Balaam spoke over the people of God, his mouth found only words of blessing.

Balak, naturally, was furious. His bad intentions had been bent by God into something good. But he really should have seen it coming: Balaam had even told Balak that he couldn't say anything that differed from what God wanted—and it was obvious by now that God had chosen to bless Israel. No amount of bribery, threats, or anger could change Balaam's mind. Sure, Balaam was wrong to even consider cursing Israel, but his obedience ultimately compelled him to do what was right.

Maybe you're looking at your current situation and

wondering why God hasn't "fixed" things exactly the way you asked Him. If so, stop and think, *Is that something He'd actually do? Does my request violate one of His rules?*

God will never alter His own plan to make it fit your plan. He has always been in control, so when He says no, His decision will be for your good.

WHEN GOD SAYS NO, DOES IT SEEM LIKE A
PUNISHMENT TO YOU? WHY MIGHT THIS ACTUALLY
BE THE KINDEST RESPONSE SOMETIMES?

A TIME TO REMEMBER

"You must commit yourselves wholeheartedly to these commands that I am giving you today. Repeat them again and again to your children. Talk about them when you are at home and when you are on the road, when you are going to bed and when you are getting up."
DEUTERONOMY 6:6–7 NLT

Years had passed since the people had exited Egypt through the Red Sea. Each day, God had openly guided them, using a pillar of clouds by day and a pillar of fire by night. Who else had this kind of GPS? Who else drank divinely granted water in the desert? No one.

The Israelites accepted His gifts, of course. But they apparently lacked the attention span or memory to turn this acceptance into gratitude. So instead, they forgot God's goodness.

Remembering often requires intentionality—that's why God gave a list of key trigger phrases to prevent His people from forgetting His works. "Commit yourselves," He ordered. "Repeat" the commands and "talk about them." The Israelites weren't doing that. . .and neither are many Christians today, it seems. In the minds of many, God is like more like a refueling station or spiritual snack store than a beloved family member.

When you find yourself drifting from God's plan for your life, take His three commands to heart: commit yourself to following His rules, repeat what you know to loved ones, and talk about God's plan everywhere you go. (Truthfully, that last part is rarely easy.)

Once you notice all the ways God creates miracles from calamities, you'll experience a gratitude you won't soon forget.

DO YOU EVER FORGET GOD IN IMPORTANT DECISIONS OR WHEN CONVERSING WITH YOUR FAMILY? DO YOU EVER ASK FOR GOD'S HELP, THEN IGNORE OR FORGET HIS REPLY? HOW CAN YOU DO BETTER?

WHOSE GOODNESS?

Understand, then, that it is not because of your
righteousness that the LORD your God is giving you this
good land to possess, for you are a stiff-necked people.
DEUTERONOMY 9:6 NIV

By providing them a new home, God was finally fulfilling His promise to Israel. The people to whom He'd given the promise—Abraham, Isaac, and Jacob—didn't enjoy it during their lifetime. That privilege fell to their descendants.

These people, however, had done very little but complain. They spoke unkindly about their leaders while engaging in activities God had forbidden. If God's goodness were based on a merit system (it's not), then these people would have been disqualified ages ago. But if that had happened, God's promise wouldn't have been fulfilled. . .and God always keeps His promises.

So He gave a home to the people who didn't deserve even His basic kindness. Their bad became good—not because *they* were good, but because God certainly was.

God's goodness to you may have nothing to do with your behavior or choices. His goodness falls on you simply because He's good. He doesn't pick and choose which farmer gets rain—it falls on those who love God and those who don't (see Matthew 5:45).

This isn't meant to discourage you. Rather, it's to remind you that even when we don't deserve it, God's goodness guarantees that our bad days will bring forth good.

If you're grateful for this good news, let go of your rebellion and rejoin God in a journey. He's been waiting for you to walk with Him.

DO YOU EVER GROW JEALOUS WHEN BAD PEOPLE RECEIVE GOOD THINGS? HOW MIGHT YOU GROW TO TRUST GOD'S JUDGMENT ON WHO AND WHEN HE BLESSES?

REBELLION'S TABLE

*[God said,] "This people. . .will forsake Me and break
My covenant that I have made with them."*

DEUTERONOMY 31:16 SKJV

God didn't have to predict something so obvious—even Moses
could see that the people still wore rebellion like a favorite shirt.
This was a time of transition. God was about to walk before the
people into the promised land, knowing they'd quickly forget
Him. He knew they'd turn their backs on Him. He knew they
were stubborn. But He also knew they couldn't go on living
like nomads. . .that they craved a roof over their heads. . .that
they needed a home.

Moses had led them this far; now it was time for Joshua
to take up his mantle. But God wanted Moses and Joshua to
understand that this transition wouldn't be a "happily ever after"
ending. It would be a catalyst for renewed rebellion.

Yet as Moses finished one of his final addresses to the people,
he said, "Set your hearts to all the words that I testify among
you this day, which you shall command your children to be
careful to do—all the words of this law. For it is not a vain thing
for you, because it is your life" (Deuteronomy 32:46–47 SKJV).

God could see the outcome, yet He still offered the people

a remedy—if they would just pay attention. The people had no one but themselves to blame for their misfortune, but God remained in control. Even more, He kept inviting them to return to Him from their seat at rebellion's table.

This is the same God who calls you each day. He knows when you'll rebel, but that won't stop Him from urging you to leave behind your hesitation and follow Him.

WHY DOES GOD STILL OFFER GOOD OUTCOMES—
TO INDIVIDUALS AND NATIONS—EVEN WHEN HE
KNOWS CERTAIN ONES WILL REBEL? WHY DO YOU
THINK MOSES SAID GOD'S LAWS ARE LIFE?

REBELLION'S GREENHOUSE

[God said,] "This is my command—be strong and courageous! Do not be afraid or discouraged. For the LORD your God is with you wherever you go."

JOSHUA 1:9 NLT

Joshua was the newly installed leader of Israel. He came into the position knowing that the people had hearts that were not bent in God's direction. They were quite pleased to be getting a new home, but they'd also been spending too much time entertaining fear.

Joshua started the way Moses had ended: by reminding the people not to fear. God, of course, knew before the words were spoken that Joshua's command would be ignored. After all, the people were like unruly sheep, wandering away from their divine shepherd and tuning out His voice. Nothing about their attitude had changed. Yet God still promised to lead them to the promised land, where they'd plant their rebellion for a future harvest.

God had walked with so many—from the first man, Adam, to every human who was born thereafter. And every single person had proven beyond doubt that they were incapable of completely trusting and obeying Him. Therefore, God had a whole lot of "subverting bad choices" to do. He tirelessly worked—on both national and personal levels—to demonstrate His resourcefulness to a nation that needed multiple lifetimes to notice.

For you, however, God's actions have already been written. You don't have to spend a lifetime wallowing in uncertainty. Fear and discouragement are useless wherever God works.

WHY DO YOU THINK IT'S EASIER TO GIVE IN TO FEAR EVEN WHEN TRUSTING GOD WILL ALWAYS MAKE MORE SENSE? WHO BENEFITS MOST WHEN YOU'RE DISCOURAGED BY FAILED DECISION-MAKING?

YOUR FUTURE STORY

[Rahab said,] "Please swear to me by the LORD that you will show kindness to my family, because I have shown kindness to you. Give me a sure sign."

JOSHUA 2:12 NIV

God had promised to give the land to the Israelites. And now a two-person covert advance team was passing beyond the walls of Jericho to gather intel about the city. Local soldiers were closing in, however, and capture was all but guaranteed. The spies' recon mission was starting to look like a one-way trip.

That's when these two men met a woman from Jericho named Rahab, who seemed to have greater faith in God's plan than most of the Israelites did. Certain that God would give the city to Joshua, she hid the two men and asked them to ensure her safety when Israel came to claim Jericho.

God honored that request. Sure, Rahab was about to be displaced from her home, but God would turn this bad situation into good by sparing her life, right? Yes. . .and then He did even more. Rahab would become the mother of Boaz, who would meet and marry a widow named Ruth. These two were the parents of Obed, the father of Jesse. And Jesse was the father of David, the most famous king of Israel. And as we all know,

David's line eventually led to Jesus.

Clearly, Rahab's faith was a history-defining event, even though it may not have seemed like it at the time.

You never know how your decision to trust God today will impact future generations. You may not even live to see the outcome, but God will keep working long after you've breathed your last.

HOW CAN RAHAB'S STORY EXPAND YOUR VISION OF GOD'S WORK BEYOND TODAY OR EVEN BEYOND YOUR LIFE? HOW IMPORTANT TO YOU IS GOD'S FUTURE PLAN FOR YOUR PRESENT DECISIONS?

PROTECTION CITIES

The LORD also spoke to Joshua, saying: "Speak to the children of Israel, saying, 'Appoint cities of refuge for yourselves, of which I spoke to you by the hand of Moses, that the slayer who kills any person unintentionally and unwittingly may flee there. And they shall be your refuge.'"

JOSHUA 20:1–3 SKJV

Ever heard the phrase "innocent until proven guilty"? God introduced this concept.

In the promised land, there were to be six "cities of refuge": Kedesh, Shechem, Hebron, Bezer, Ramoth, and Golan. (The number would later grow.) Their purpose? Those who'd accidentally killed someone could travel to them for protection. There they would be given a chance to prove their innocence.

There were special rules that those seeking refuge would need to follow. In some cases, the innocent individuals would have to live in one of these sanctuary cities for the rest of their lives. Inconvenient? Yes. Lifesaving? You bet. If an innocent person didn't go, the family of the individual who was unintentionally killed could seek vengeance.

These cities were just another way God proved that He can redeem even the worst misfortunes. What's more, they illustrate how important it is that we show mercy before justice, never letting a bad situation inspire bad decisions. Since God doesn't jump to conclusions, neither should we.

WHY DO YOU THINK GOD INCORPORATED THESE CITIES INTO HIS PEOPLE'S CULTURE? DO YOU EVER WISH FOR GOD'S JUDGMENT TO FALL ON THE WORLD RATHER THAN HIS MERCY?

WARDROBE CHANGE

The Israelites did evil in the LORD's sight and served the images of Baal. They abandoned the LORD, the God of their ancestors, who had brought them out of Egypt. They went after other gods, worshiping the gods of the people around them. And they angered the LORD.

JUDGES 2:11–12 NLT

Joshua led the people until he was well past one hundred years of age. But not long after his death, the people forgot the journey that led them to their new home. They forgot the stories of idol worship in the wilderness and their slavery in Egypt. They forgot how God sent Joseph into Egypt to save the lives of their ancestors. They forgot all the even older stories that should have been on their hearts, minds, and lips.

God had predicted the people would turn their backs on Him—and they did. They no longer followed His commands, choosing to glean their spiritual advice from the surrounding pagan nations rather than from the God of their fathers. Therefore, even though God was clearly the only one worthy of their worship, the people chose to follow the non-god, Baal, along with a host of more "interesting" gods. They tried out deities like wardrobe accessories. Whatever seemed the most dazzling captured their attention—and their hearts—for a time.

God was the only reason they were still alive, yet they chose to worship lifeless idols instead. So God was angry.

Unlike humans, God doesn't act impulsively on His anger. But this time, He had to do something. . .so He began the process of correcting their direction. All their godless endeavors would fail. They needed to realize that God's good outcomes aren't a license for bad behavior.

DO YOU FIND IT EASY TO BE DISTRACTED FROM GOD? HOW CAN YOU KEEP YOUR FOCUS ON HIM?

AN INVITATION DECLINED

Barak said to [Deborah], "If you go with me, I will go; but if you don't go with me, I won't go."
JUDGES 4:8 NIV

Deborah was a messenger for God, and she had a very specific message for the military hero Barak. After telling the heralded soldier that their adversary, Sisera, was about to be defeated, she delivered the most important part of God's message: "I will. . .give him into your hands" (Judges 4:7 NIV).

Barak had never heard of a surer outcome. All he needed to do was show up, play his part, and witness the defeat. But somehow, Barak found a way to mess it up: he refused to go if Deborah didn't go with him. Consequently, the title of war hero would be passed along to someone unexpected.

God was still in control and the enemy would still be defeated, but the spotlight was shifting from Barak to a woman named Jael. You might never have heard of Jael if Barak had accepted God's invitation to a ringside seat. As it turned out, she was the one who defeated Sisera.

God often asks you to be part of His plan, but even if you turn Him down, it will not stop that plan from being accomplished. Rather, the blessing that was intended for you might suddenly belong to someone else.

Make no mistake—Barak was blessed in knowing that God had dealt with his country's foe. But he also lived with the regret of knowing he had turned God down.

HAVE YOU EVER "TURNED GOD DOWN" ON AN INVITATION TO OBEY? WHAT WAS THE OUTCOME? WHY IS IT ENCOURAGING TO KNOW THAT GOD'S PLAN WILL STILL HAPPEN, NO MATTER WHAT?

A SELF-DESCRIBED PIP-SQUEAK

The LORD looked on [Gideon] and said, "Go in this strength of yours, and you shall save Israel from the hand of the Midianites. Have I not sent you?"
JUDGES 6:14 SKJV

The people of Israel felt abandoned. . .and honestly, they had it coming. God had rescued them repeatedly, and they repeatedly responded by being grateful for maybe the rest of the day. (That's what it seems like to us as readers, anyway.)

Still, in Israel's darkest hour, God sent a man named Gideon. By Gideon's own admission, he was a nobody. He was just trying to protect a harvest from the marauding Midianites. So when God's messenger angel showed up, this self-described pip-squeak gave the angel an earful. He basically told him in verse 13, "God is with us, you say? Then what's happening? Where are His miracles He performed for our fathers? No, God has forsaken us."

Talk about a pessimist! Like Moses, Gideon was certain God had the wrong man. He even seemed to doubt the angel was truly an angel after all. But God took the time to convince this insecure man that He'd chosen him to rescue Israel. And if Gideon had any doubts, all he needed to remember was the one who'd sent him.

Because of Gideon, Israel's tragedy was about to become a triumph.

God chooses the most unlikely people to bring order to chaos. So if He chooses you to bring His message to someone, don't chew Him out. Don't think He's got the wrong man. Simply ask God to help you step out. . .and watch Him do the impossible.

HAVE YOU EVER COMPLAINED ABOUT A BAD SITUATION
AND THEN, BECAUSE OF YOUR INSECURITIES,
REFUSED TO BE A PART OF THE SOLUTION? WHAT
DID YOU LEARN? WHAT ARE YOU LEARNING?

WITHOUT DEFENSE

*Gideon took ten of his servants and did as the
LORD had commanded. But he did it at night
because he was afraid of the other members of his
father's household and the people of the town.*

JUDGES 6:27 NLT

When we read about Gideon yesterday, he was hiding and
making excuses—a fact that didn't stop God from sending
him out as a warrior. But before he faced any Midianite, he
had to face his own people. His relatives had set up altars to the
non-god, Baal, and Gideon was to tear them down and build
a new altar to God.

When the people discovered this "desecration" and learned
who did it, a violent, angry mob stormed to the house of
Gideon's father to call for Gideon's death. But Gideon's father,
Joash, apparently also had unexpected courage. He essentially
told the crowd that if Baal were offended, then he should
defend himself.

Father and son—Joash and Gideon—discovered a courage
with God that they didn't have on their own. Both men had
to be emboldened to stand up for truth and watch God work
in unforeseeable ways.

You may find yourself in the spiritual doldrums, stuck in your bad circumstances and no longer looking for a way out. If so, ask God what He wants you to do. If He gives you an assignment, He'll make sure you're equipped to do the work. As He's proven over and over again, God is bigger than any problem, obstacle, or objection.

HAVE YOU EVER BELIEVED THAT ONLY SOME MEN CAN BE USED BY GOD? HOW DOES IT IMPACT YOU TO READ ABOUT QUIET MEN WHOM GOD ASKED TO BE MIGHTY?

TOO MANY MEN

His friend responded, "This can be nothing other than the swift sword of Gideon son of Joash, the Israelite. God has given the Midianites and the whole camp into his hands."

JUDGES 7:14 NIV

Gideon didn't start out brave, yet God asked him to rescue His people from the Midianites. And along the way, Gideon had second thoughts—lots of them. But at last, Gideon now had an army of thirty-two thousand men at his camp. *Maybe I can do this after all*, he must have thought.

Then God told every soldier who was afraid—two-thirds of Gideon's army—to go home. . .which they gladly did. Gideon was no doubt shaken and confused. After all, hadn't he himself felt afraid, hiding in a barn not so long ago? *Oh well, I still have ten thousand men.*

But God wasn't finished. He said there were *still* too many men. Whenever Gideon's soldiers stooped to drink water, most laid face down on the shore and drank directly from the surface. Three hundred, however, drank from cupped hands. "Keep those men," God said.

Just like that, ninety-seven hundred brave, able bodied men went home that day, leaving what must have looked like the

69

most pathetic army in history.

But God knew fear would consume the Midianites, so winning a battle with three hundred men wouldn't be a problem for Him. This modest crew stood on the hillside, waiting for Gideon to give the word. When he did, they broke the three hundred jars covering their lit torches. The flash of light was accompanied by a quick noise: the sound of trumpets and the shout, "A sword for the Lord and for Gideon!" (verse 20 NIV). In fear, the Midianites fought back—but against themselves. They handed over the victory to God's small army.

Once again, God had used the worst of odds to achieve the greatest of results.

WHY WOULD GOD USE SUCH AN UNUSUAL SITUATION
TO ACHIEVE A VICTORY? DOES THIS STORY IMPACT
YOUR IDEAS ABOUT HOW GOD WORKS?

THE QUESTION OF KINGS

In those days there was no king in Israel.
JUDGES 18:1 SKJV

One simple statement: *There was no king in Israel.* Was this bad news or good? After all, Israel's judges up to that point had been a mixed bag. Some were worth following; others, not so much.

But through it all ran the destructive currents of idol worship and invading armies. The people would follow the judges for a while. . .and then rebel shortly thereafter. Maybe it was because the judges weren't taken seriously. Or maybe people were just doing what they thought was important. Judges 17:6 makes it clear: "Every man did what was right in his own eyes" (ESV). To Israel, not even God Himself—the one who'd rescued them time and again and gave them their land as a gift—was important enough to follow.

Truthfully, the people did need a king, someone who would rein in the Israelites' self-destructive habits. But that wasn't their biggest problem—as shown by the fact that their cycle continued long after God gave them the king they wanted. Instead, their true issue lay in their lack of willingness to allow God—who'd offered to fulfill that role already—to rule in their hearts.

It's a condition all men face. But take heart—good can

come from this too. Once we recognize our need for God as our king, we'll learn He's far more qualified than any human being—including ourselves—ever could be.

WHY IS A LEADERLESS LIFE A GOOD STARTING POINT
FOR GOD'S GUIDANCE TO BEGIN? HOW IS GOD'S
FAITHFULNESS CONNECTED TO HIS GOODNESS?

A MOVE THAT
CHANGED HISTORY

Ruth replied, "Don't ask me to leave you and turn back.
Wherever you go, I will go; wherever you live, I will
live. Your people will be my people, and your God will
be my God. Wherever you die, I will die, and there
I will be buried. May the LORD punish me severely
if I allow anything but death to separate us!"
RUTH 1:16–17 NLT

Four family members—Elimelech, his wife Naomi, and their two sons, Mahlon and Kilion—were driven from Israel by a famine. After leaving Bethlehem and settling into life in Moab, Elimelech died. This was a crushing blow to Naomi, but her two sons soon found wives in their new land. Thus, life continued with her expanded family.

The Bible doesn't let us know how Elimelech died, nor does it tell us how both of her sons died later. . .but it does tell us that Naomi was suddenly filled with an intense longing to return to her home country. Maybe things were better in Bethlehem. Maybe she wanted to connect with old friends. Either way, she planned to leave Moab and go home. . .alone.

One daughter-in-law, however, refused to leave Naomi's

side. You've probably heard of Ruth. She too was suffering the wound of losing her own husband, but somehow her heart remained tied to her husband's family.

Naomi described herself as bitter—an understandable reaction to the loss of the most precious people in her life, along with the loss of her homeland. So how did God use this heartbreak to create healing? Through Naomi's determination to return to Bethlehem. Upon her return, her daughter-in-law Ruth, who'd likely never have gone to Israel on her own, would meet and marry a man named Boaz. . .and later become the great-grandmother of Israel's famed King David.

HAS GOD EVER USED YOUR OWN NEGATIVE EMOTIONS TO BRING YOU INTO A PLACE OF HEALING? IF SO, WHY IS IT STILL WISE TO REJECT OR WORK THROUGH YOUR NEGATIVE EMOTIONS WHENEVER THEY APPEAR?

A PRAYER OF
THE DESPERATE

Her husband Elkanah would say to her,
"Hannah, why are you weeping? Why don't
you eat? Why are you downhearted?
Don't I mean more to you than ten sons?"
1 Samuel 1:8 niv

Hannah's bad day was having unexpected consequences. As she prayed for a son, the priest Eli thought she was drunk, and her husband, Elkanah, was naive enough to think his love could replace her desire for a son. In her desperation, Hannah rightfully concluded that the only one who would listen was also the only one who could help. So with tears of desperation and a voice likely ragged with grief, she prayed the prayer of the childless. And God, who comes close to the brokenhearted, heard her grief—along with the vow she made.

"Lord Almighty," she said, "if you will only look on your servant's misery and remember me, and not forget your servant but give her a son, then I will give him to the Lord for all the days of his life" (1 Samuel 1:11 niv). And no matter how flippantly or apathetically her husband and the priest treated her spiritual bargaining, God didn't overlook it.

God granted the request of the desperate, and this desperate woman fulfilled her promise. She would welcome the birth of her son and be his mother for the rest of her life—but he would become God's servant for the rest of his. When that little boy was old enough, Hannah brought him to Eli, the priest, and left him to serve God.

All prayers are unique because the individuals who pray them are unique. Therefore, God's answers are usually unique as well. Hannah's prayer stemmed from her unique need, and God replied by giving her a God-honoring son named Samuel. Later, Samuel would work in the temple and even anoint kings for service.

And this good outcome all started with prayer.

IS PRAYER YOUR NATURAL REACTION TO DESPERATE SITUATIONS? HOW CAN YOUR TIMES OF DESPERATION LEAD YOU CLOSER TO GOD'S PURPOSE?

REJECTED AND REPLACED

*The LORD said to Samuel, "Listen to the voice
of the people in all that they say to you, for they
have not rejected you, but they have rejected
Me, that I should not reign over them."*

1 SAMUEL 8:7 SKJV

Three days ago, you read about Israel's odd dilemma—they had no king. The people looked to the nations surrounding them, all of which had kings, and experienced social envy. *Why should we be any different?* they thought. Soon, voices became insistent. The people wanted—then demanded—a king. Even when reminded that this king would take their sons and place them in military service, the people still began to shout, "We want a king!"

Samuel, now an adult and the prophet of Israel, knew the people were not thinking clearly. He knew having a king would mean a greater burden for the people. But no amount of reason would stop them from wanting to "keep up with the Joneses."

Samuel was against the idea of crowning a king, and he took his objections to the Lord. Surprisingly, God comforted the prophet by telling him that the people's desire stemmed from a rejection of God's leadership. Because they preferred a human leader over their divine Savior and King, God told Samuel to simply give them what they wanted.

Israel's unique leadership structure was coming to an end. Samuel still opposed the idea of a king, but he would obey God and anoint Israel's first two monarchs. The first king (Saul) would be proof enough that the people would have been much better off with God as their leader. This knowledge may have brought some back to God. Others would continue drifting further away.

The time of kings had come, and so had the official beginning of the nation's spiritual downfall. Yet even for these people who thought they no longer needed Him, God was still in control.

HOW CAN ENVY IMPACT YOUR CLOSENESS TO
GOD? WHAT USUALLY HAPPENS WHENEVER
YOU REFUSE TO ALLOW GOD TO LEAD?

ENCOURAGEMENT
AND WARNING

*[Samuel said,] "Be sure to fear the L*ORD *and faithfully serve him. Think of all the wonderful things he has done for you. But if you continue to sin, you and your king will be swept away."*
1 SAMUEL 12:24–25 NLT

The prophet Samuel was at the end of his life, and he was finishing the way he started. His mother had dedicated him to God, and God had used Samuel throughout his life. He anointed Israel's first king, even when he was convinced it was a bad idea.

Now at the end of his life, Samuel gave the people words of encouragement: *Remember God.* But he also gave a warning, essentially saying, "If you continue to break God's rule, things will not go well for you. . .or your king."

Samuel was giving the people two clear options. The first would remind the people of God's faithfulness and lead to success. The second would cloud their vision, causing them to stumble blindly in spiritual darkness.

The cracks in King Saul's leadership were obvious to Samuel. And even though Samuel recognized the promise in David as

Israel's second king, the prophet knew that even David would never be a perfect choice. After all, nobody could rescue the people like God could.

Samuel knew that the Israelites' choices would not only impact their own lives but influence the decisions of the king. After all, both the follower and the leader were human, prone to poor choices. Those choices had consequences—devastating and far-reaching ones.

God was in control when men broke His rules. He was in control when they failed to lead properly. And He remained in control when mankind made their worst decisions.

Even today, God is still in control, changing lives on a worldwide and personal level all at once—with one change often impacting the other. Have you let Him change you?

WHY DID SAMUEL SAY THE FATE OF A NATION WAS NOT TIED EXCLUSIVELY TO THE ONE WHO LED THE NATION? HOW MIGHT SAMUEL'S WARNING CHANGE YOUR VIEW OF LEADERSHIP?

WISE ENOUGH
TO BRING GOD

"Now what have I done?" said David. "Can't I even speak?"

1 Samuel 17:29 niv

David was anointed king as a young man, but his leadership would wait until King Saul's passing. In this time of waiting, David spent his time on hillsides with sheep. To us, this doesn't sound very king-like; to God, David's humble position qualified him all the more.

David was the youngest of his brothers, and he often had the job of traveling to the front lines of war to bring his brothers gifts from home. On one such mission, he overheard a giant, fearsome Philistine warrior named Goliath taunting the soldiers of Israel. Even worse, no one seemed brave enough to stand up to him. So David asked questions.

Maybe it was because David's brothers were jealous of him—like Joseph's had been—or maybe it was just a typical sibling spat. Regardless, David's oldest brother, Eliab, was annoyed by his question, and he even suggested that the only reason David showed up was to see a good show. But David was having none of it. "What have I done?" he cried. "Can't I even speak?"

Eventually, David's questions led to answers. Those answers

led to an idea. And that idea led to David facing Goliath on the battlefield as Eliab and his other brothers watched from the sidelines. Why? Because David wasn't afraid to bring God into his planning. He heard someone making fun of God, so he asked God for help in bringing him down.

In response to Goliath's familiar taunts, David broke the cycle by proclaiming, "You come against me with sword and spear and javelin, but I come against you in the name of the LORD Almighty, the God of the armies of Israel, whom you have defied. This day the LORD will deliver you into my hands" (verses 45–46 NIV). And that's exactly what happened.

David's story proves that defeat can give way to victory whenever we ask God to do the miraculous.

HOW MIGHT THE OPINIONS OF OTHERS NEGATIVELY AFFECT YOUR DECISIONS? WHEN GOD ASKS YOU TO DO SOMETHING, WHY IS CONFIDENCE THE BEST RESPONSE?

A RESTORATION PROJECT

Abner communicated with the elders of Israel,
saying, "In times past you sought for David to
be king over you. Now then, do it. For the LORD
has spoken of David, saying, 'By the hand of My
servant David I will save My people Israel.' "
2 SAMUEL 3:17–18 SKJV

Abner immersed himself in the leadership culture of Israel. He was quick to side with whomever he considered a winner. He was street-smart and ruthless.

Abner had sided with King Saul's son, Ish-Bosheth, who would become the king of Israel for a short time. When Ish-Bosheth became a disappointment to Abner by bringing up an issue Abner didn't wish to confront, Abner took a pro-David agenda to Israel's leadership. They agreed David should rule all Israel, not just Judah.

Abner confronted a fast-running man named Asahel, who chased Abner in response. Abner warned the runner to stop chasing him, but Asahel refused. . .so Abner took his life.

Asahel had been a brother to Joab, a leader in David's army. Therefore, Joab waited for what he thought was the right time for revenge. And in a rash and impulsive moment that would disrupt everything, Joab decided to kill Abner.

This caused strain in the plan to make David ruler of all Israel. Some thought David had been involved in the plot, but David's grief over the loss of Abner convinced most people otherwise.

This was supposed to be a happy time for David—a time of great celebration. Yet Abner's actions had set off a fatal, calamitous string of events.

Chances are, you can relate to Abner's story—minus the murderous parts, hopefully. Yet even as Abner's choices spiraled into chaos, God was working behind the scenes to restore order. . .just as He's always done.

AS THOSE AROUND US—AND EVEN WE OURSELVES, PERHAPS—MAKE HORRIBLE CHOICES, DOES IT EVER SEEM LIKE GOD ISN'T IN CONTROL? HOW IS THIS THINKING FLAWED?

HE DID NOT SEE
THAT COMING

The king then asked [Ziba], "Is anyone still alive from Saul's family? If so, I want to show God's kindness to them."

2 SAMUEL 9:3 NLT

King Saul had a son named Jonathan, who had a friend named David. By the customs of kingship observed in the nations around them, Jonathan should have been Israel's next king. Samuel, however, had anointed David to take on that responsibility. Interestingly, Jonathan was all for this idea. So when David learned Saul and Jonathan had both died, you can imagine his grief. David didn't lose a rival in Jonathan—he lost a friend.

Once David took the throne, he asked if there was anyone left of Saul's family. The people's attention had been consumed by revenge and violence, and David wanted to change things up—he wanted to show kindness. So when the king discovered Mephibosheth, Jonathan's disabled son, David brought him into his palace and took care of him. Mephibosheth and his son Mica ate at the king's table and were treated with respect.

David's commander, Joab, had pursued revenge when he took the life of Abner, but David craved something different. He wanted to avoid the lawlessness that had run rampant in the days of the judges. So he simply offered kindness and friendship to a man whom, according to the conventional wisdom of the nations around him, he should have killed.

Isn't that how we as Christians are supposed to live? When the world insults, hates, and takes revenge, we encourage, love, and forgive, looking for ways to help our enemies. God will always remain in control, and He's always willing to help you control your emotions. . .thereby bringing about His best outcome.

HOW CAN YOU SHOW THAT GOD IS IN CONTROL OF YOUR CHOICES? WHY DOES CONTROLLING YOUR EMOTIONS LEAD TO GREATER CONTROL?

WHEN YOU ARE THAT MAN

David burned with anger against the man and said to
*Nathan, "As surely as the L*ORD *lives, the man who did*
this must die! He must pay for that lamb four times
over, because he did such a thing and had no pity."

2 SAMUEL 12:5–6 NIV

King David was a man after God's heart. He defeated a giant who taunted God's people. He wrote many of the psalms that people still memorize today. He waited on God for a promised kingdom.

But David wasn't perfect. One day, when he was distracted, he saw a beautiful woman and conspired to commit adultery with her. To cover it up, David ensured that her husband would die on the front lines of battle. Then? David took this woman, Bathsheba, to be his wife.

He was the king, so nobody was willing to question him. . .except for Nathan the prophet. When Nathan arrived, the king welcomed him and listened as he launched into a story about two men: a rich man who had plenty of sheep and a poor man who had one lamb, which he loved like family. When the rich man had guests over, he told his kitchen staff to make a meal, but instead of choosing from his own large flock, he instructed them to go to the poor man's house and take his beloved lamb.

David, furious at the rich man's actions, responded with the words in today's passage. When the king asked the name of this pitiless miser, Nathan had a four-word reply: "You are the man!" (verse 7 NIV).

Nathan isn't mentioned much in the Bible. He doesn't have a book of his own, and he's mostly remembered for this one interaction with David. But his simple story changed King David's life, bringing perspective to his selfish downward spiral. There would be consequences, of course, but there would also be forgiveness.

God didn't change the fact that David had sinned. . .but he did alter his outcome by changing David's heart.

WHAT GOOD OUTCOMES HAVE HAPPENED TO YOU EVEN WHEN THE DISASTER WAS YOUR FAULT? HOW DID GOD'S MERCY ALTER YOUR FUTURE DECISIONS?

HE CHOSE WISELY

In Gibeon the Lord appeared to Solomon in a dream by
night. And God said, "Ask. What shall I give you?"
1 Kings 3:5 skjv

Today's verse marks the beginning of a story—one of many in
the Bible—in which God flipped the script, transforming a bad
situation into a blessing.

Solomon had just inherited the crown from his father,
David. Even though his older brother had briefly contested him
for it, the struggle was now over, and Solomon sat on the throne.

Solomon, no doubt overwhelmed by the task of leading a
nation, mulled over how he would rule the people. That's when
God posed a single question to him: "What shall I give you?"

Given how taxing Solomon's job would be, the greatest
thing he could think to ask for was. . .wisdom. If Solomon
could know how to lead the people and make difficult choices,
then all his other desires would fall into place. God was pleased
with Solomon's request and was more than happy to grant it.
God liked this answer so much, in fact, that He told the king
that he would also receive riches and honor.

From the very beginning, Solomon's kingdom was estab-
lished on his willingness to allow God to lead the leader.

Solomon was interested in God's plan, and he deeply trusted God's wisdom in carrying out His plan. Solomon wanted access to that kind of wisdom.

WHAT WOULD BE THE VALUE IN ASKING GOD FOR SOMETHING HE ALREADY WANTS TO GIVE YOU? WHY IS WISDOM A BETTER GIFT THAN RICHES OR HONOR?

THE WEATHERMAN

The LORD said to Elijah, "Go to the east and hide by Kerith Brook, near where it enters the Jordan River. Drink from the brook and eat what the ravens bring you, for I have commanded them to bring you food."

1 KINGS 17:2–4 NLT

Elijah was the most accurate weatherman ever. He said it would be dry and sunny for a few years, and he was right. When he later followed this up by predicting rain, his forecast was spot-on. He should have been in line for "Meteorologist of the Millennium." Of course, Elijah was a prophet. He only told people what God had told him. . .and God is never wrong.

Still, it was probably hard for Elijah to give this forecast. People tended to laugh at him first and get upset when he was proven correct. King Ahab, however, never thought the prophet was funny. He called him a troublemaker, and he even went so far as to send out a search party for the prophet to force him to bring rain back into the forecast. But since God had made the call, that wasn't Elijah's decision to make.

Clearly, it was a bad day to be a prophet. God was the one who created the drought, but everyone took their anger out on the messenger.

God protected Elijah, however, by sending him to a brook, where ravens brought him food and the brook's water quenched his thirst. When the brook dried up, God sent Elijah to a specific widow's house, where he was miraculously fed until God brought the rain again.

While Elijah was a guest in this home, the woman's child died. So God gave Elijah yet another set of instructions. Elijah obeyed. . .and this time, instead of a drought happening, a boy came back to life.

These were bad times for everyone, including Elijah and the widow. But because God kept working, life was preserved through the suffering. Good always exists with God, come rain or shine.

WHEN DID YOU LAST WONDER IF GOD'S GOOD ANSWER WOULD COME? WERE YOU SURPRISED BY HIS REPLY?

THE RETURNING RAIN

[Obadiah] said, "What have I sinned, that you would deliver your servant into the hand of Ahab, to slay me?"
1 KINGS 18:9 SKJV

Obadiah loved God but worked for a bad king. His boss was King Ahab, who—along with his wife, Queen Jezebel—always seemed to make the worst possible decisions. One day, the king threw a tantrum because he wanted a vineyard that the owner wouldn't sell. So how did Jezebel respond? By having the owner killed, of course.

On other occasions, Jezebel also killed many of God's prophets. So imagine Obadiah's surprise when he bumped into Elijah one day, and Elijah told him to let Ahab know he wanted to meet him! Today's verse gives his panicked response. Surely, Elijah would just slip away again like he had when the rain had stopped falling. If that happened, it'd be certain death for Obadiah. But Elijah calmed Obadiah's fears by saying, "As the LORD of hosts lives, before whom I stand, I will surely present myself to him today" (verse 15 SKJV). That prediction was just as correct as his sunny forecast.

When Elijah later met the king on Mount Carmel, he addressed the crowd: "How long will you halt between two opinions? If the LORD is God, follow Him, but if Baal, then follow him" (verse 21 SKJV). No one knew quite how to respond. Maybe that's because since they had started following Baal, the land had dried up and the people were hungry.

On that mountaintop, Baal's priests were embarrassed by their god's inaction. The *real* God, however, showed up in a display of fire and rain. The lack of rain had gotten their attention, so God's gift of rain found an appreciative audience. Situation: controlled.

WHEN HAVE YOU BEEN A BIT LIKE OBADIAH, WONDERING IF SHARING THE TRUTH COULD HURT YOU? WHY DOES GOD SOMETIMES GO TO GREAT LENGTHS TO GET YOUR ATTENTION?

THE PRACTICAL PROPHET

One day the widow. . .came to Elisha and cried out,
"My husband who served you is dead, and you know
how he feared the LORD. But now a creditor has
come, threatening to take my two sons as slaves."
2 KINGS 4:1 NLT

Elijah chose someone to take his place as a prophet in Israel—someone with the very similar name of Elisha.

One day, a widow told Elisha about her family's financial condition. Her two sons' futures were at stake. If she couldn't raise the money her creditors demanded, her sons would become slaves.

When Elisha asked what the woman had to sell, the only thing she could think of was a small bottle of olive oil. Surely, this bottle wasn't enough. But Elisha told the widow to borrow any container she could find and then pour her olive oil into one of them. When that one was full, she poured into a second, then a third, until every container was filled with olive oil. Finally, Elisha told the women, "Now sell the olive oil and pay your debts, and you and your sons can live on what is left over" (verse 7 NLT).

Another day, as Elisha passed through a town, a couple

befriended Elijah and allowed him to stay in their home. He told this couple they would have a son. . .and they did. Another time, he purified a contaminated water source. He also made a pot of poisoned stew fit to eat. And in a miracle that may sound familiar, he once fed a hungry crowd with a single bag of grain and twenty loaves of barley bread, saying, "Everyone will eat, and there will even be some left over!" (verse 43 NLT). The people left satisfied.

This whirlwind trip through some of Elisha's greatest hits proves how God can take the common stresses of life and infuse them with His good results.

DO YOU HAVE TROUBLE REMEMBERING GOD'S POWER ON THE BAD DAYS? WHAT ARE WAYS IN WHICH HE'S HELPED YOU THAT WEREN'T IMMEDIATELY OBVIOUS?

A KING'S STRESS

As soon as the king of Israel read the letter, he tore his robes
and said, "Am I God? Can I kill and bring back to life?
Why does this fellow send someone to me to be cured of his
leprosy? See how he is trying to pick a quarrel with me!"
2 KINGS 5:7 NIV

King Jehoram was likely sick with worry. The king of Syria had
sent a simple letter saying, "I am sending my servant Naaman
to you so that you may cure him of his leprosy" (verse 6 NIV).

As it turns out, the Syrian king had initially learned about
Naaman from a servant girl who worked for Naaman's wife.
She'd mentioned a prophet in Israel who could help. . .but the
Syrian ruler had sent his letter to Israel's king instead.

The king was not a doctor, and we have no record that he
ever healed anyone. So his exasperation in today's verse makes
perfect sense. However, Elisha—the prophet whom the servant
girl had been talking about—had the answer: he told the king,
"Have the man come to me and he will know that there is a
prophet in Israel" (verse 8 NIV).

Naaman was already on the move. When he arrived, Elisha
sent out a messenger to give him his long-awaited healing
instructions: wash in the Jordan seven times.

Naaman felt cheated. Why hadn't Elisha seen him personally? And wasn't the water at his home cleaner than the Jordan River? Discouraged, Naaman prepared to go home, but one of his own servants convinced him to give it a try. After all, it *might* work.

It did.

The king's bad day ended because Elisha stepped up to remind everyone that God was at work in Israel. Naaman's bad day ended when his skin disease left him. And all along, Elisha knew that bad days don't exist whenever God is the solution.

HOW DID THE ANXIETY AND FRUSTRATION OF NAAMAN AND THE KING CONTRAST WITH ELISHA'S ATTITUDE? HOW MIGHT THIS STORY ENCOURAGE US TO FOLLOW GOD'S DIRECTIONS?

TRANSFER OF POWER

Jehoash was seven years old when he began to reign.
2 KINGS 11:21 SKJV

The grandmother of Jehoash (also known as Joash) would have hardly qualified for the title of "Grandmother of the Year." When her son, King Ahaziah of Judah, died, she decided she wanted to rule. The only thing standing in her way were a few pesky heirs to the throne. . .so she ordered them all killed. Now that her competition was removed, she took the throne as queen.

But Ahaziah had an infant son whom she overlooked. Jehosheba, the queen's daughter and the sister of the recently deceased King Ahaziah, took this infant and hid him, placing the boy under the care of a priest named Jehoiada. And that's how Jehoash, the child, came to know God's law.

The queen, smugly thinking her rule was secure, was in for a rude awakening. Seven-year-old Jehoash, as today's verse says, would soon be installed as king. Naturally, the new king and his grandmother didn't have a warm reunion.

Sometimes unexpected rivals can throw a monkey wrench into our plans. This was true from the queen's perspective, obviously, but think of how stressful it must have been for young Jehoash! He likely didn't understand the full implications until later. He was sheltered, hidden away, and forbidden from living like other boys. His life would be in danger if the queen ever found out about him, and he was thrust into royal responsibilities at a very young age.

None of this escaped God's attention, however. More than any earthly king (or queen), God Himself remained on the throne, pulling the strings to achieve His greater plan.

HAVE YOU EVER STRUGGLED WITH A RIVAL? WHAT DID YOU LEARN? DID YOU SEE THIS RIVAL AS AN ENEMY?

PURSUING THE GOOD

Hezekiah trusted in the LORD, the God of Israel.
There was no one like him among all the kings
of Judah, either before or after his time.
2 KINGS 18:5 NLT

Hezekiah was an ambitious reformer. When he took over as king of Judah in his mid-twenties, he effectively declared, "Enough is enough." Second Kings 18:4 says, "He removed the pagan shrines, smashed the sacred pillars, and cut down the Asherah poles" (NLT).

There was even a relic dating back to before the people took possession of the promised land. Moses had fashioned it in the wilderness, and God had allowed it to protect the people from snake bites. Eventually, however, the Israelites had named this relic Nehushtan, and it had become just another idol to take God's place. Hezekiah ordered it smashed.

The Israelites had had a regrettable past, but God was using Hezekiah to tear it all down. Second Kings 18:7 says, "The LORD was with him, and Hezekiah was successful in everything he did" (NLT).

Hezekiah also found success in military might. He faced adversaries and, with God's help, won battle after battle. Why?

Because he trusted God.

Hezekiah's trust was put to the test, however, when the king of Assyria sent some of his staff to threaten Hezekiah and the people of Judah. It seemed to be working. . .until the king redirected his faith toward God. The people likely thought Hezekiah should give in to the king of Assyria's demands, but Hezekiah wanted what God wanted. So God chose to help.

Today, let Hezekiah be your role model. Refuse to take the path of least resistance. God will always be in control—it's just easier for you whenever you choose not to stand in His way.

DOES IT EVER SEEM PREFERABLE TO ASK GOD FOR
FORGIVENESS THAN PERMISSION? HOW DOES HEZEKIAH'S
SELFLESS AMBITION DISPROVE THIS NOTION?

REBUILDING THE WALLS

[Nehemiah said,] "Hanani, one of my brothers,
came from Judah with some other men, and I
questioned them about the Jewish remnant that had
survived the exile, and also about Jerusalem."
NEHEMIAH 1:2 NIV

Jerusalem was mostly abandoned when the people were taken captive by Babylon. Nehemiah was one of those people. He lived in a place far from home and had a job tasting drinks for the king—practically a death sentence, given that the entire point of his job was to notify the king of any poisons in his cup. . .by dying before the king drank it.

One day, Nehemiah's brother sent him some disheartening intel on the status of Jerusalem. The city was less than a shadow of its former glory—the people were mostly gone, the walls were destroyed, and rubble was everywhere. It was impossible for Nehemiah to hide his emotional devastation.

The king asked for the details, putting Nehemiah in a precarious spot. If the king thought his concern was ridiculous, then Nehemiah would be guilty of wasting the king's time—an offense potentially punishable by death.

To Nehemiah's relief, the king was sympathetic. Even more

surprisingly, the king agreed to help. He would send Nehemiah to Jerusalem, provide protection on the way, then pay for the proper wall-building materials. Soon, Nehemiah was marshalling a workforce to get the job done. God had prepared the way, and this rebuilding would kickstart the people's return from exile.

Maybe you're dissatisfied with where you are. Maybe you believe you were made for something more. And maybe God does have bigger plans for you—only He knows what they might be. The only question is. . .are you willing to let God use you to do something new?

WHY DO YOU THINK NEHEMIAH CARED SO MUCH ABOUT JERUSALEM'S CONDITION? NAME THREE OF YOUR BIGGEST GOALS: WHY ARE THEY IMPORTANT TO YOU? ARE YOU SEEKING GOD'S HELP TO ACCOMPLISH THEM?

THE TURNABOUT

*And Haman said to King Ahasuerus, "There is a certain
people scattered abroad and dispersed among the people
in all the provinces of your kingdom, and their laws are
different from all people and they do not keep the king's laws.
Therefore it is not for the king's profit to put up with them."*
ESTHER 3:8 SKJV

This is a story of a king, a selfish man, and a third man who
pointed out the selfishness he saw.

The selfish man, Haman, convinced King Ahasuerus that
he needed to deal forcefully with a group of people living in
his kingdom. Their laws, he said, were just too strange. The
real reason for his hatred, however, was that he didn't like
Mordecai, the man who'd pointed out his selfishness. Haman
had a history of being petty, but he really crossed a line this
time: to get his revenge, he planned to eliminate every member
of Mordecai's family.

Mordecai's day couldn't have been going any worse.

What Haman didn't know, however, was that the queen
was related to Mordecai. Mordecai convinced Esther to talk
to the king, who decreed that Mordecai's family were allowed
to defend themselves against this killing spree.

Once more, God had taken a despicable scheme and transformed it into an example of His goodness.

The world is filled with people who are willing to hurt anyone in their path to get their way. But God is still in the business of changing outcomes. Sometimes those outcomes take a while to arrive, but God always provides the grace to endure until His answer comes.

God will always be bigger than your worst day, no matter how bad it may be.

HAVE YOU EVER USED DIFFICULT MOMENTS AS AN EXCUSE TO THROW A PITY PARTY? WHY IS IT IMPORTANT TO REMEMBER GOD'S GOODNESS IN THE MIDST OF YOUR WORST EXPERIENCES?

NOTICED

The LORD asked Satan, "Have you noticed my servant Job? He is the finest man in all the earth. He is blameless—a man of complete integrity. He fears God and stays away from evil."
JOB 1:8 NLT

Job was a great example of a man who followed God. Nobody expected him to do the wrong thing. He led a fairy-tale life, and nothing but good things happened to him. Everyone noticed how much God had blessed him.

Suddenly, however, Job's worst day arrived. His children died, his livestock were destroyed, and his health immediately declined. Nobody could have seen this coming, and those who knew him jumped to a quick, incorrect conclusion: Job had finally done something wrong. Even his three friends, who showed up to sit with him in his days of struggle, quickly changed their tune from empathy to accusation.

Despite the best efforts of his friends and even his wife— who told him to curse God and die—Job was still striving to maintain his integrity.

Job's struggles, of course, were being caused by forces beyond anyone's control.

God had actually boasted of Job's integrity to Satan, who

dared the Lord to remove the man's protections. Interestingly, God agreed. . .but not without placing limitations on what Satan could do. God was convinced that Satan was wrong—that Job's integrity would remain.

God didn't initiate Job's bad circumstance, but He allowed it. Through it all, He never took back the love He had for Job. Despite Job's bafflement at his trials, he stands as a model for all those who seek to remain faithful through hardship.

Sometimes unexplainable things happen. But often what seems unfair is just preparation for God's future blessing.

DO YOU EVER THINK GOD'S BLESSINGS HAVE TO BE IMMEDIATELY VISIBLE? WHY IS IT INCORRECT TO SEE A LACK OF VISIBLE BLESSING AS A SIGN OF SPIRITUAL FAILURE?

GOD'S CONSISTENT INTERVENTION

The LORD said to me, "Do not say, 'I am too young.'
You must go to everyone I send you to and say whatever
I command you. Do not be afraid of them, for I am
with you and will rescue you," declares the LORD.
JEREMIAH 1:7–8 NIV

Jeremiah didn't have much life experience when God called him. As the son of a priest, he may have spent time considering his future. But suddenly, God came to him and said, "Before I formed you in the womb I knew you, before you were born I set you apart; I appointed you as a prophet to the nations" (verse 5 NIV). Jeremiah's reply was essentially "I can't speak very well and I'm too young." Maybe his response reminds you of Moses, who had similar concerns when God called him. But just as God overcame Moses' personal objections, He would do the same for Jeremiah by giving him the words he needed to speak.

Jeremiah would find himself ridiculed and abused—even tossed into a cistern at one point for his obedience. But he just couldn't resist sharing God's message, even when he tried.

Whether we see it or not, God is always in control from the beginning of every story. Each story in this book—as well as each story in our lives—is different, yet the outcome is always in God's favor. God's intervention isn't just the stuff of legends and ancient stories; it's just as real today as it was for the people in the Bible.

God loves working in the lives of His followers. When He gets involved, bad becomes good, despair turns to hope, and fear is replaced by courage.

WHY IS AGE NEVER A PROBLEM AS LONG AS A PERSON IS WILLING TO FOLLOW GOD'S PLAN? HOW CAN YOU ENCOURAGE OTHERS WHO MAY FEEL AS IF GOD IS ASKING THEM TO DO SOMETHING SPECIAL?

A DIET CHANGE

Daniel determined in his heart that he would not defile himself with the portion of the king's food or with the wine that he drank. Therefore, he requested of the prince of the eunuchs that he might not defile himself.
DANIEL 1:8 SKJV

Like Jeremiah, Daniel was young when he was confronted with a hard decision. He was one of many who were taken captive to Babylon, and the king had picked him as one of his employees. This job involved something that sounds great: eating the king's best food. But it was food that God had outlawed, so Daniel simply refused.

Daniel was in no position to make demands. Instead, he gently requested that a different meal plan be provided. Daniel's preference was based on his relationship with God—so if *God* wanted Daniel to have a new option, it would happen. The prince of the Babylonian eunuchs determined that Daniel could eat his diet of choice—for a limited time. If Daniel didn't appear as healthy as those who ate the king's food, then the deal was off.

But that's not what happened. Daniel looked better, felt better, and chose to follow God with greater courage. In the end, his meal request became his standard diet.

In this age of all-you-can-eat buffets and fully stocked grocery shelves, a meal preference might not seem like a big deal. As the king's captive, however, Daniel had no alternate choices. Denying the king would have been suicide. . .had God not been walking before this faithful man, once again preparing a way where it seemed none existed.

If you have a conviction that your circumstance threatens to violate, don't automatically assume there's nothing you can do about it. Pray, seek God's best, and wait for His answer.

WHAT WAS AT STAKE IN THIS STORY,
BEYOND DANIEL'S MEAL PLAN? HOW MIGHT HIS
STORY INSPIRE YOU TO STAND YOUR GROUND?

THEY WOULD NOT KNEEL

"There are some Jews—Shadrach, Meshach, and Abednego—
whom you have put in charge of the province of Babylon.
They pay no attention to you, Your Majesty. They refuse to serve
your gods and do not worship the gold statue you have set up."
DANIEL 3:12 NLT

This wasn't the first time these three men had stirred the Babylonian pot with their faithfulness. In fact, they had joined Daniel in the food plan you read about yesterday. And now, Shadrach, Meshach, and Abednego were refusing to follow the king's new law, which said "that at the time you hear the sound of the cornet, flute, harp, lyre, stringed instruments, dulcimer, and all kinds of music, you fall down and worship the golden statue that Nebuchadnezzar the king has set up" (verse 5 SKJV).

These three knew that God didn't want His people to worship anyone but Him. He was the only one worth worshipping. So when the music played and everyone else bowed low, these three men—quite literally—stood out. Even after the king gave them a second chance, they still kept standing.

The punishment was overkill: a furnace was heated far hotter than usual, and the three men were thrown into the blaze. Not even the soldiers who tossed the lawbreakers inside survived the heat that blasted from the furnace doors.

But suddenly, the angry king saw something curious: these three men were just casually walking around in the flames! He called them to come out, and they did so without harm.

What should have been a really bad day for these men was flipped on its head when God stepped in. Because of their unshakable faith, everyone who saw the miracle—even the king—had a change of heart that day.

When you do the right thing, there are no consequences greater than God's plan, provision, and purpose.

ARE YOU SOMETIMES TEMPTED TO FOLLOW CULTURE'S DEMANDS OVER GOD'S? WHEN HAVE YOU SEEN GOD REWARD SOMEONE'S CHOICE TO FOLLOW HIM ABOVE ALL?

NICE KITTY

They went to the king and spoke to him about his royal decree: "Did you not publish a decree that during the next thirty days anyone who prays to any god or human being except to you, Your Majesty, would be thrown into the lions' den?"
DANIEL 6:12 NIV

This is a story of jealousy and retribution. Daniel was much older than he had been when he asked for a change in meal plans. He had been elevated to the role of the kingdom's second-in-command, much to the chagrin of the other men who were part of the country's leadership. After all, Daniel was a captive, not a native-born Babylonian. Why should he be given a place of honor?

These jealous men sought ways to trap Daniel, but the only thing they could find was that Daniel always prayed to God. What if they could get the king to agree that everyone had to pray to him? What if they made the penalty for disobedience a night in the lion's den?

The king must not have been thinking of Daniel when he accepted their suggestion. And by the time he realized this law would spell death for Daniel, it was too late—the decree was written in such a way that it couldn't be changed.

Sure enough, Daniel was soon caught praying. He was convicted and sentenced. But none of this took God by surprise. As the end of this story reveals, not even ferocious lions can hurt the man with faith in God.

The Lord is aware that the decisions of others will often cause problems in your life. But no matter how dead-set your enemies may be on derailing your faith, God will always find a way to triumph. He'll be with you, even in the lion's den.

HAVE YOU EVER SPENT A NIGHT IN A METAPHORICAL DEN OF LIONS? WHAT DID YOU LEARN? WHY IS IT IMPORTANT TO KNOW THAT IN YOUR WORST MOMENTS, GOD'S GOODNESS AND MERCY WILL FOLLOW YOU?

FRESH VISION

*The word of the LORD came to Jonah, the son of Amittai,
saying, "Arise, go to Nineveh, that great city, and cry against
it, for their wickedness has come up before Me." But Jonah
rose up to flee to Tarshish from the presence of the LORD
and went down to Joppa. And he found a ship going to
Tarshish, so he paid the fare and went down into it, to go
with them to Tarshish from the presence of the LORD.*
JONAH 1:1–3 SKJV

Jonah had a straightforward career: each time God gave him a message, he delivered it, no questions asked. He was a prophet, and prophets didn't get to pick their audience or destination.

One day, however, God gave Jonah a message. . .and Jonah said no.

Jonah's destination should have been Nineveh, but he booked a passage to Tarshish instead. God wanted him to extend a chance for mercy, but Jonah craved justice.

God, however, has a way of maneuvering life events to help His children see with fresh vision where they should go. So Jonah's boat trip out of town was interrupted by a raging storm. Eventually, he found himself on a three-day timeout. . .inside the stomach of a big fish.

You've probably guessed by now that Jonah's bad day was of his own making. But even after Jonah miraculously left the fish's stomach and preached repentance in Nineveh, he still chose rebellion as his first response. When the people followed God, Jonah became angry. He wanted mercy for himself and justice for the Ninevites.

It's always better to agree with God so that you can recognize His good outcome.

WHY IS REFUSING GOD'S DIRECTIONS NEVER A GOOD IDEA? IF GOD WERE TO USE YOU TO BLESS YOUR ENEMIES, WOULD YOU BE HAPPY OR ANGRY?

SILENCING DOUBT

In the time of Herod king of Judea there was a priest named Zechariah, who belonged to the priestly division of Abijah; his wife Elizabeth was also a descendant of Aaron.

LUKE 1:5 NIV

Zechariah was a descendant of Aaron. Therefore, he was a priest—that's what Aaron's family did. He knew God's laws, read His words, and taught His way. But when confronted with the unthinkable, Zechariah had questions.

He'd been praying for a son. But Zechariah and his wife were old, having lived most of their lives without conceiving. Still, though, he prayed. When the angel Gabriel showed up to say that God had heard his prayers and would give him a son, the priest—after getting over his initial terror—said, "How can I be sure of this? I am an old man and my wife is well along in years" (verse 18 NIV).

So why had Zechariah been praying for a son if he didn't believe it was possible? Was it simply a habit? Had he promised his wife he'd keep praying. . .without really believing God would answer? Was the idea simply too remarkable to comprehend?

Zechariah received a timeout for his disbelief. God would indeed bless him with a son, who would grow up to become John the Baptist. This son would prepare the way for Jesus' ministry. But until the baby arrived, Zechariah would be unable to speak.

After their boy was born, Elizabeth said he would be called John. Since this wasn't a family name, people had questions for Zechariah. In response, he wrote on a tablet—since he couldn't speak—"His name is John" (Luke 1:63 NIV). Immediately, he was no longer mute. Imagine all the things he had to say!

Keeping faith in God can be hard, especially when your situation seems impossible. But even when doubt creeps in, God continues to show that He's in control. You just have to step aside and wait for Him to move.

CAN YOU IDENTIFY WITH ZECHARIAH?
WHY IS IT HARD TO TRUST GOD SOMETIMES,
EVEN WHEN WE KNOW HE CAN DO ANYTHING?

NO SENSE

*Joseph, to whom [Mary] was engaged, was a righteous
man and did not want to disgrace her publicly,
so he decided to break the engagement quietly.*

MATTHEW 1:19 NLT

Joseph was a hard-working man who likely never fled from his problems. But at the moment described in today's verse, he could see no option other than damage control. His fiancée was pregnant, and he wasn't the dad. They were engaged. . .but marriage now seemed out of the question. So Joseph, while being as kind as possible to Mary, decided to break off the engagement.

His choice was entirely understandable—commendable, even. It made no sense to marry the girl. It seemed she had been unfaithful, so why marry a woman whose affections lay elsewhere? And Joseph didn't want to commit himself to raising someone else's child.

However, that's when Joseph got the inside story. Against all odds, this news changed his misfortune into a miracle: the child Mary would bear would be the Son of God. Joseph chose to believe the report. How do we know that? Because he went through with the marriage. Joseph had never been one to back down from a problem. . .especially not when God was offering His assurance.

God has always asked people to believe in the impossible. His ways are so different from ours, His plans so impenetrable, that we often couldn't understand them even if we could see them. But His ways are also perfect. So your situation right now, no matter how painful or hopeless it may seem, is building toward the fulfillment of His unbreakable plan.

HOW CAN WE EVEN BEGIN TO BELIEVE IN THE IMPOSSIBLE?
WHY IS TRUSTING GOD ALWAYS THE WISEST CHOICE?

A NIGHT IN THE FIELD

In the same country there were shepherds abiding in the field, keeping watch over their flock by night.
LUKE 2:8 SKJV

You can imagine that most nights were the same for the shepherds. The sheep bleated but stayed within the sheepfold, predators lurked just out of sight, and the shepherds fought their drowsiness to protect the sheep. These men likely had a campfire that offered protection, warmth, and a pleasant distraction. The sunsets and stars were probably beautiful, which was one perk of working the night shift in the field.

Fear breached the camp, however, when an angel appeared. After telling them not to be afraid, the angel declared that an unprecedented event had happened in town. God was controlling the message, ensuring it was received by this group of common men.

History doesn't record the shepherds' names—or even whether they brought gifts. We can only imagine their response to seeing the child. Their presence, however, drives home the humility of Jesus' birth. He was born in a stable, not a palace, and visited by lowly shepherds.

And this was all because God delivered a message.

Think back to the time you first heard God's message of salvation. Maybe it was from a preacher, a friend, or even a radio or television program. God wanted you to know about His Son, Jesus, so He arranged a time and place for you to hear His message in a way you could understand.

God's care in delivering His soul-saving news should drive us to proclaim, like the angels did in verse 14, "Glory to God in the highest."

HOW ARE YOU PAYING ATTENTION TO THE GOOD NEWS GOD HAS FOR YOU? HAVE YOU ACCEPTED THIS NEWS?

WAITING TO MEET

*Simeon was there. He took the child in
his arms and praised God.*
LUKE 2:28 NLT

Both Mary and Joseph had been visited by angels who'd told them the significance of their baby boy. But perhaps there were times when He seemed like any other baby. Maybe in those moments, it was easy to forget that He would always be more.

Eight days after Jesus was born, Mary and Joseph presented Jesus in the temple in Jerusalem. While there, they met a man who'd been waiting a very long time to meet this child. God had promised Simeon that he would see the Messiah, and he'd waited most of his life for His arrival.

Now, as the older man gazed into the face of God's Son, he knew this was the one. To Mary and Joseph's amazement, he prayed: "Sovereign Lord, now let your servant die in peace, as you have promised. I have seen your salvation, which you have prepared for all people. He is a light to reveal God to the nations, and he is the glory of your people Israel!" (verses 29–32 NLT). Simeon could not imagine anything more important than meeting the Savior of the world. And now that he had, he could die in peace, knowing that God had kept His personal promise.

The truth is, we hear nothing more about Simeon. But his story may make us wonder if the Son of God has impacted our lives as deeply as He did that old man's. After all, meeting Jesus and developing a friendship with God is no minor life event—it's the greatest, most fulfilling thing that could happen to you. It should reorder your priorities and change your future.

It should be easy to say with Simeon, "I have seen Your salvation, which You have prepared for all people."

DO YOU EVER SEE GOD'S GIFT OF SALVATION AS AN ENTITLEMENT AND NOT AS A GIFT OF IMMENSE VALUE? ARE YOU AS EXCITED AS SIMEON WAS TO RECOGNIZE AND RECEIVE GOD'S GREATEST GIFT?

WELCOME TO THE CITY

The boy Jesus stayed behind in Jerusalem,
but they were unaware of it. Thinking he was in
their company, they traveled on for a day.
LUKE 2:43–44 NIV

Although not yet a man, Jesus spoke like one. He'd gone to Jerusalem with Mary and Joseph, but when they left the city to go home, Jesus remained in the temple. There, He listened to the religious leaders and asked them questions—astonishing questions, coming from someone so young.

While Jesus was discussing the finer points of God's law with men much older than Himself, Mary and Joseph were just learning that He wasn't in their homeward-bound group. Were they upset with Him for vanishing? Were they kicking themselves for not checking sooner? Did they think Jesus was being disobedient?

We don't know the answers to any of these questions. . .but really, we don't need to. Jesus' discussion with the religious leaders was foreshadowing a far greater truth: His future ministry in Jerusalem.

God's good plan included Jerusalem. That was where Jesus was presented to God at eight days of age, it was where He was now impressing teachers at twelve years, and it would be where people would cheer. . .and then jeer. . .during His final hours. The same city whose walls Nehemiah had rebuilt long ago—whose history included a line of miracles, prophets, and good and wicked kings—was about to take center stage in God's great rescue plan.

Jesus taught here, once as a boy and later as an adult. And all along, God was giving Him the words. These words have long-since reached beyond this pivotal city, where they continue to impact humankind today.

HAVE YOU EVER CONSIDERED CERTAIN PEOPLE—
MAYBE EVEN YOURSELF—AS OFF-LIMITS FROM GOD'S
MESSAGE OF LOVE? HOW DOES THE GOOD NEWS THAT
JESUS SHARED IN JERUSALEM IMPACT YOU?

HE STAYED IN CONTROL

Jesus, being full of the Holy Spirit, returned from the Jordan and was led by the Spirit into the wilderness, being tempted for forty days by the devil. And in those days He ate nothing.
LUKE 4:1–2 SKJV

God's always in control. Apparently, however, Satan never got the memo.

The devil knew Jesus was God's Son. He knew Jesus came to earth as a man. He knew men get hungry. So when Jesus spent forty days in the wilderness without food, Satan thought it was the perfect time to see if God's control could be broken.

Nobody can take advantage of humanity's weaknesses and deepest longings better than Satan can. So the devil must have believed that if he could offer Jesus the things that most humans want, then maybe Jesus would simply give in. Maybe, since Jesus was hungry, all the devil would have to do would be to gently remind Him of His connection to God—of His power to turn stones into bread. But Satan had overlooked one fact: Jesus was well aware of this power. His life consisted in God instead of food. Plus, He had nothing to prove to the enemy.

Then the adversary went big, suggesting that Jesus worship him in exchange for all kinds of power on earth. This plan made even less sense than the last. Jesus already owned everything! Also, Jesus made it clear that the only one worthy of worship was God, *not* this rebellious wannabe.

Finally, Satan suggested that Jesus should throw Himself from Jerusalem's temple, trusting in God to send Him angelic assistance. But once again, Jesus saw through the scheme. God isn't some wish-granting genie, nor can He be bossed around—He's holy and worthy of all honor. Jesus had no reason to test Him needlessly. He already knew God's perfect plan.

WHY DOES IT MATTER THAT JESUS STAYED IN CONTROL?
WHY DOES IT MATTER THAT SATAN LOST THIS BATTLE?

A GREAT DAY FOR FISHING

When [Jesus] had finished speaking, he said to Simon, "Now go out where it is deeper, and let down your nets to catch some fish."
Luke 5:4 nlt

Simon was an experienced fisherman. No one needed to tell him how to do his job. . .until one night when, despite Simon's best efforts, he couldn't catch a single fish. Repeatedly, he tossed his net and pulled it back. Empty, every time.

He knew fish, but he couldn't control them or wish them into a net. But all night, he'd worn himself out trying. When morning came, he must have felt as if he had wasted his time. He washed the nets that morning, no doubt looking at them with a touch of disdain.

That's when Jesus asked him if He could get on his boat and preach to a gathering crowd from the Sea of Galilee. Simon agreed and listened as Jesus spoke. After the message, as the people made their way home, Jesus gave Simon (later called Peter) some rather unorthodox advice about fishing.

Maybe Simon was grateful. Or maybe he was annoyed but decided to simply humor Jesus, thinking it wouldn't hurt to try. Either way, he replied, "We worked hard all last night and didn't catch a thing. But if you say so, I'll let the nets down again" (verse 5 NLT).

A strange thing happened whenever Simon tried pulling the nets back: they were so full, he had to call for help! Simon's helpers were brothers named James and John. . .and they would join Simon that day in following Jesus.

They saw, in the simple act of fishing, that Jesus controlled what they couldn't. Even today, He continues to demonstrate this ability for all of us.

HOW DOES IT ENCOURAGE YOU TO KNOW THAT JESUS CAN CONTROL WHAT YOU CANNOT? WOULD THESE MEN HAVE FOLLOWED JESUS HAD THEY NEVER KNOWN HIS POWER?

HE WAS WILLING

*While Jesus was in one of the towns, a man came along
who was covered with leprosy. When he saw Jesus,
he fell with his face to the ground and begged him,
"Lord, if you are willing, you can make me clean."*

LUKE 5:12 NIV

Today's verse describes a man who recognized Jesus' power. He
was desperate, and desperation made him bold.

Jesus had been preaching to many people in many different places, but this man was forbidden all human contact. He
had a wasting skin disease called leprosy. He was "unclean," so
he should have been outside the city, proclaiming his status
when people walked his way. Those with his condition usually
died alone.

Yet on that day, this unclean and wounded man said something astonishing to Jesus: "Lord, if you are willing, you can
make me clean." This man didn't ask Jesus if He was powerful
enough to help or say that he'd heard good things about Him.
No, he simply bowed his face to the ground and proclaimed
his belief that Jesus could heal him—if He was willing.

This man's request was free from disrespect and full of
honor. What was Jesus' response? Jesus reached out His hand

and *touched* the man. "I am willing," he said. "Be clean!" (Luke 5:13 NIV). The leprosy immediately left the man.

There was no mandatory quarantine. No waiting. This man was instantly, miraculously, and utterly clean.

What if we all had this kind of trust? What if we absolutely believed that God could take care of our needs? God doesn't want us to make arrogant demands, but He does want us to believe He can do the impossible—if He's willing.

HOW MUCH FAITH DO YOU HAVE IN THE GOD WHO CONTROLS EVERYTHING? HOW CAN WE CONFIDENTLY REQUEST THINGS FROM GOD WHILE RESPECTING HIS ANSWER?

SAY THE WORD

*The centurion sent friends to [Jesus], saying to Him,
"Lord, do not trouble Yourself, for I am not worthy
that You should enter under my roof. Therefore I
did not think myself worthy to come to You. But say
in a word, and my servant shall be healed."*

LUKE 7:6–7 SKJV

The centurion was a Roman soldier, not a Jew. In fact, the Jews probably saw him as an enemy, even though he'd helped build their synagogue. They hated the Romans, who had power but not necessarily control over Jewish hearts and minds.

Nevertheless, men reported to this centurion. He gave orders and expected them to be followed. He understood, therefore, that Jesus—the overseer of reality itself—could simply give a command and something incredible would happen.

So this unnamed soldier made a critical decision. He had a servant who was sick, and he didn't want to see this servant die. So he asked some of the Jews he'd helped to go and ask Jesus to heal his servant. Jesus agreed to come. . .but the soldier demurred. He was unworthy, he explained, for Jesus to visit him personally. All Jesus had to do was say the word, and his servant would be healed.

This was a rare response, even for those who knew the Lord. And for a Roman who had no close ties to God? Unthinkable! Yet this Roman soldier recognized where real power came from. He knew who was really in control. Jesus said of the man, "I have not found so great faith, no, not in Israel" (Luke 7:9 SKJV). Then Jesus healed the servant—from a distance.

You aren't an outsider. You've always been welcome to ask for divine assistance. Even when it makes no sense, you can trust God's willingness to help. Believe God can control what no one else can.

WHY IS IT IMPORTANT TO RECOGNIZE THAT GOD HAS MORE POWER THAN US? WHY IS THIS CENTURION'S STORY ALL THE PROOF WE NEED TO KNOW GOD CAN HELP?

KNOCK IT OFF
AND CALM DOWN

The disciples went and woke [Jesus] up,
shouting, "Master, Master, we're going to drown!"
LUKE 8:24 NLT

Some of Jesus' disciples were fishermen. For them, He had already proven He controlled the fish—now it was time for them to see Him control the weather.

The twelve had likely been in significant storms in the past, but none were as fearsome and tumultuous as the storm they experienced in Luke 8. But while these men were wondering if they would live through the night—while the waves crashed and water sprayed over their battered boat—Jesus slept.

We don't know how many disciples approached Jesus. All we know is that when they woke Him, they were convinced of their imminent demise. In response, Jesus told the wind to knock it off and the waves to calm down. Both obeyed the Son of God, and all became quiet. Then Jesus turned to His still-quaking followers and said, "Where is your faith?"

The men didn't respond to this question. They were too busy asking, "Who is this man? When he gives a command, even the wind and waves obey him!" (Luke 8:25 NLT).

When storms arise, whether figurative or real, have you ever been able to silence the wind with a mere "Knock it off and calm down"? Of course not. You aren't in control of your storm. . .but you can know the God who is. You don't have to fear the wind and waves—you just need to have faith in the God who's greater than them both.

That's what Jesus' disciples discovered two thousand years ago. And that's what you can discover today.

DO YOU FIND IT ALL TOO EASY TO GIVE IN TO DESPAIR?
WHY IS FEAR OFTEN OUR KNEE-JERK REACTION TO TROUBLE?

FED

[Jesus] replied, "You give them something to eat."
LUKE 9:13 NIV

It's easy to say the words, "God said it, I believe it, and that settles it." It sounds really faithful. . .until our faith is actually put to the test.

Jesus' twelve disciples had recently watched Him tell the wind and waves to shape up. You'd think this event would have profoundly impacted their faith, but it wasn't long before they needed another lesson.

People had come one day by the hundreds and thousands to hear Jesus speak. They'd listened to His message and watched as He healed many. Eventually, however, some of the more practical-minded disciples pointed out that the crowd was growing hungry. It was probably best to wrap things up and send everyone home for supper.

Jesus' response was puzzling: "You give them something to eat." How could they give what they didn't have? Apparently, they'd looked before asking Jesus, and all they could find was one boy's lunch of fish and bread. Maybe the disciples thought this would convince Jesus to end the day sooner than expected so that the people could find food. But Jesus was about to do something far more spectacular.

He began with an act the disciples should have thought of right away—He prayed. Then He snapped the fish apart and pulled the bread into bits. Jesus told His disciples to distribute the food to the people as He continued to snap and pull, snap and pull. Little became much, and the hungry were fed. And to top it all, *twelve baskets* of leftovers remained!

For the Son of God, a boy's lunch was more than enough to feed an entire multitude. The disciples needed a reminder that their God could do the impossible. Do you?

WHY IS IT INCORRECT TO THINK THAT GOD ASKS TOO MUCH OF US? WHAT CAN WE DO TO IMPROVE OUR TRUST IN GOD?

THEY WENT AHEAD

*After these things the Lord appointed seventy others
also and sent them two by two before His face into
every city and place where He Himself would go.*

<small>LUKE 10:1 SKJV</small>

We all know about the twelve disciples. These were the men closest to Jesus—the ones you read about in the New Testament. They have names like John, James, Peter, and Thomas. They're recognizable. Most have stories we're all familiar with.

Yet in Luke 10, we read of seventy other followers who were closer to Jesus than most. His circle went beyond just twelve men. There were dozens of people who stuck with Jesus and learned from Him as He traveled from place to place.

Jesus gave these seventy people a job: go ahead of Him into the towns He would visit and tell the people they met about their long-awaited Messiah. That way, these citizens wouldn't have to worry about meeting a total stranger—they would have first heard all about Jesus from those who knew Him personally. They would know how life-changing His message was.

Just like John the Baptist, these seventy people were Jesus' advance team, sent to set the stage for the main event: His arrival. Jesus was coming with a message of healing and life.

The old way of thinking—the hardness of people's hearts—was about to give way before Jesus' soul-saving news.

Jesus' seventy followers were willing to recognize His control and go where He sent them. Consequently, God used them to do amazing things. Are you as willing as they were?

HOW FAR ARE YOU WILLING TO GO TO FOLLOW GOD'S DIRECTION? HOW MIGHT YOU FOLLOW HIM MORE INTENTIONALLY?

BARNS, BIRDS, AND BAD NEWS

Turning to his disciples, Jesus said, "That is why I tell you not to worry about everyday life—whether you have enough food to eat or enough clothes to wear."
LUKE 12:22 NLT

What's one sure sign that you aren't in control? Fear. If you could control every situation, circumstance, and struggle, then fear would be an alien emotion. If God were not certain of His every decision, then He'd also experience fear. But He's never been afraid. Not once.

In Luke 12, Jesus told His disciples the story about a rich man who was driven by fear so strongly that he chose to hoard rather than trust God. And after the story, Jesus instructed His followers not to worry about their next meal or even what they'd wear tomorrow. Otherwise, they'd end up like the rich man, having more than enough but always seeking more.

Then Jesus took it a step further. He pointed out some common birds and said that they have no barns. Rather, they have to rely on God to take care of them, which God always does.

Jesus knew that it's impossible for worry to make us live longer. And the more time we spend obsessing fruitlessly over our problems—big or small—the less likely we'll be to remember the one who's actually in control.

God has repeatedly said He loves us—something He hasn't said about any of the animals. And given that He still cares for the smallest birds, what a comfort that should be!

IS IT EVER HARD FOR YOU TO REJECT WORRY? WHY MIGHT IT HELP TO KNOW THAT GOD HAS NEVER EXPERIENCED FEAR?

JUST A LITTLE BIT LOUDER

Those who led the way rebuked [the blind man]
and told him to be quiet, but he shouted all the
more, "Son of David, have mercy on me!"
LUKE 18:39 NIV

. . . .

"What do you see?" Maybe the blind man in today's verse asked that question to those around him. He'd heard of the miracle man named Jesus who was passing through—of His power to heal those who were hopelessly sick. If only he could talk to this man, perhaps he could see.

When the man was certain Jesus was near, he called out, "Jesus, Son of David, have mercy on me!" (Luke 18:38 NIV). This caused ripples in the crowd. The blind man likely had no trouble with his hearing—he was well aware that people thought he was being rude and improper. But put yourself in his shoes: if you were in a similarly desperate situation, would you stay quiet because that's what others expected you to do? Or would you cry out to God for help?

The blind man chose the latter. Once more, and perhaps with greater gusto, he cried, "Son of David, have mercy on me!" Miraculously, Jesus stopped. The blind man had the full attention of the Son of God. Jesus wanted to know this man's specific request. Was it a comfortable life with no need to beg? Money? A long life? No, this man was clear: he wanted to see. And when Jesus healed him because of his faith, this man did more than say thanks—he immediately followed Jesus through the streets of Jericho.

Thankfully for the blind man, neither he nor the crowd who wanted him to be quiet was in charge that day. That role belonged to Jesus—the only one who could turn this man's tragedy into an opportunity for praise.

WHY IS IT IMPORTANT TO NOTE THAT JESUS RESPONDED WHEN THIS MAN SHARED HIS NEED? HOW DOES THIS REFUTE THE OFT-QUOTED (BUT UNBIBLICAL) STATEMENT, "GOD HELPS THOSE WHO HELP THEMSELVES"?

SINNERS WELCOME

They all murmured, saying, "He has gone to
be the guest of a man who is a sinner."
LUKE 19:7 SKJV

For Zacchaeus, friendship must have been a foreign concept. He was a short man with a long list of bad behaviors. He had a position of authority, and he used it to steal from people he should have considered family. He gathered taxes for the Roman government and then added his own unrequired fees to the receipt. He was rich, but people knew where his wealth came from—their pockets.

On the day Jesus arrived, Zacchaeus had no friends to save him a spot. . .no one with whom he could share his enthusiasm. . .no one to invite him to their group.

He had always been a man of opportunity, however, and he saw a new one that day—a tree. Climbing the tree would give him a front row seat to see Jesus walking through the city. We don't know exactly *why* Zacchaeus was so dead-set on seeing Jesus, but clearly, this man was motivated.

With crowds all around Him, Jesus looked up and invited Himself to lunch at this man's home. A guest? Had he ever had one of those? The crowd, however, was not stingy in their opinions about Jesus' new lunch companion. They thought Jesus should have nothing to do with sinners. But if that were true, how would any sinners get rescued?

Jesus did spend time with sinners—not to blend in with them but to challenge them to accept His exciting invitation to a new life. He does the same for you. He spends time with you because even when others think you're not worth the investment, He has always known better.

HOW SHOULD WE REACT TO THE FACT THAT JESUS LOVES SINNERS? HOW MIGHT GOD'S KINDNESS AFFECT YOUR OWN MINDSET TOWARD THOSE WHO NEED HIS GRACE?

A SMALL GIFT CELEBRATION

*While Jesus was in the Temple, he watched the rich
people dropping their gifts in the collection box.*
LUKE 21:1 NLT

Jesus was doing exactly what He'd done before He ever breathed air as a human—observing humanity. People fascinated Him. He loved them, yet marveled at how mixed-up they became. Sometimes they did the wrong thing for the right reasons. Other times they did the wrong thing just for the sake of doing wrong. And sometimes, they did the right thing. . .and no one else noticed.

But He noticed. He's *always* noticed.

In Luke 21 Jesus observed those who came to give financial gifts for the work of the temple. Often, people would arrive with a large donation, hoping others would see them as wealthy, generous, or both. Many treated their gift-giving like a glamorous advertisement for themselves.

However, of all the people that Jesus saw that day, it was a widow who caught His attention. She came in without fanfare, quietly dropped a couple of coins in the box, and then left. No name was given. No business card left behind. No comment to the press.

Only one man was paying attention when this woman came and went. And this man knew something no one else did: all of the biggest contributors were only giving a small portion of their wealth. . .yet the widow had given *everything*. The rich wouldn't miss their donations, yet they still craved attention for their "sacrifice." This group had great control over their wealth, but the woman simply trusted God—who deserved everything she had—and gave it all.

Therefore, the barely perceptible sound of this widow's coins hitting the bottom of the box was music to God's ears. Her sacrifice was worth celebrating—worth remembering.

WHY DOES THE CONDITION OF YOUR HEART MATTER MORE TO GOD THAN THE AMOUNT YOU GIVE? HOW CAN GIVING GIFTS TO GOD ILLUSTRATE YOUR TRUST IN HIS CONTROL?

A GARDEN BETRAYAL

Judas went to the chief priests and the officers of the temple guard and discussed with them how he might betray Jesus.
LUKE 22:4 NIV

Throughout Judas' story, we can see glaring signs of his desire for power and control. As the disciple who was in charge of the finances, he complained when he felt an extravagant gift to Jesus should have been converted to cash. Also, he seemed to believe Jesus was destined to become a great political ruler. . .which was probably why he'd chosen to follow Him. Therefore, when public opinion shifted against Jesus, Judas' opinion shifted too.

Suddenly, Judas saw himself as being on the wrong side of history. If he could just distance himself from Jesus, maybe history would forgive his former allegiance to the preacher. He was likely relieved, therefore, when he learned the religious leaders were anxious to put an end to Jesus' ministry. They were willing to do anything to stop Jesus' ministry. . .so Judas helped them.

His reward for betraying Jesus would be a small bag of coins—far better, Judas thought, than continuing to follow a disappointing Messiah. Jesus, however, had been clear about His future. It seems Judas failed to notice.

Even when Jesus revealed that someone would betray Him,

we can see Judas' deceptive mind at work. He joined the chorus of disciples who concernedly asked Jesus, "Is it me?" And in a garden just a few hours later, how did Judas finish the deed that would send Jesus to the cross? With a sign of friendship—a kiss.

Shortly thereafter, Judas realized his mistake. He returned the money he'd accepted. . .but it was too late. There was no stopping what his choices had set in motion.

What Judas didn't realize was that God was willing to use anything, even this man's despicable choice, as part of His story of redemption. Through Judas' betrayal, salvation would come to everyone who believed—including you.

HAVE YOU EVER HAD A SERIOUSLY FLAWED PLAN?
HOW HAVE YOU SEEN GOD TAKE POOR CHOICES AND
TRANSFORM THEM INTO PROOFS OF HIS GOODNESS?

FOLLOWING A VERDICT OF NO GUILT

Then said Pilate to the chief priests and to the people, "I find no fault in this man."
LUKE 23:4 SKJV

Pilate tried to prove he was in control. . .and failed. He liked his job, and he didn't want to lose it by standing up to a crowd. But still, he had spoken with Jesus and concluded He was innocent, so Pilate wanted his opinion to triumph over the crowd's. His conclusions, after all, had been correct. Surely his voice of reason would bring this agitated crowd to its senses.

But Pilate underestimated the power of envy and heightened emotion. The mob eventually prevailed, their cries for justice transforming into frenzied demands for crucifixion. All control had been lost—Pilate wouldn't have the final word.

Pilate stepped back into the shadows, assuming the people had taken control. The people themselves likely thought this was true. But they were wrong. The broken, beaten, and abused Jesus placed His hands against the rough wood of the cross, waiting for the hammer to fall. It did. And as Pilate hid inside the walls of his home, as the people's blood lust seemed to subside, Jesus gasped for air, crying out for God to forgive those who thought they were in control.

Soon, everyone went home—some still angry, others likely confused, ashamed, and numb. But that's when forgiveness arrived. As Jesus burst from the grave on the third day, offering eternal life to all, He proved He had always been in control. No one had taken His life—it was His gift. . .to you.

DOES THE MERE ACT OF AVOIDING CONFRONTATION
MEAN YOU'RE IN CONTROL? HOW MIGHT
COMPROMISE REVEAL A LACK OF CONTROL?

ROAD TRIP CONVERSATION

[Jesus] asked them, "What are you discussing
together as you walk along?"
LUKE 24:17 NIV

Two men were walking to Emmaus, just a few miles from Jerusalem. Little did they know, their road trip would be memorable—not because of the scenery but because of the man who'd walk with them and join their conversation.

This new traveler was interested in hearing what they had to say about a man who was recently executed in Jerusalem. Perhaps some of what they said came from witnessing the event firsthand. Or maybe they'd just heard the account from others who had watched the public trial unfold. Either way, one of the men was bold enough to express what so many were thinking: "We had hoped that he was the one who was going to redeem Israel" (Luke 24:21 NIV).

Perhaps, like Judas, these men assumed Jesus would be a political leader who would free them from Rome. Just that morning, they had heard, Jesus' grave had been found empty. Some reports mentioned angels surrounding the vacant tomb. These men had plenty of theories. . .but the last one on their minds was that they were talking to Jesus now.

Much as He did before His crucifixion, Jesus liked to make people think. So as He looked at these troubled men, knowing they didn't understand the truth, He asked, "Did not the Messiah have to suffer these things and then enter his glory?" (Luke 24:26 NIV).

Then the two men asked Him to stay. During the next meal, they finally recognized Jesus for who He was. . .and He disappeared. They marveled, "Were not our hearts burning within us while he talked with us on the road?" (Luke 24:32 NIV).

The meal was forgotten. The two men rushed back to Jerusalem to confirm for the disciples that Jesus was alive, having paid sin's price once and for all time. He had controlled every aspect of the recent ordeal—and had broken the power of death forever.

IS SOMETHING PREVENTING YOU FROM SEEING THE GOOD WORK GOD IS DOING IN YOUR LIFE? HAVE YOU ASKED GOD TO OPEN YOUR EYES TO HIS TRUTH?

THE PROMISE

While [the disciples] looked steadfastly toward heaven as He went up, behold, two men stood by them in white apparel, who also said, "Men of Galilee, why do you stand gazing up into heaven? This same Jesus, who has been taken up from you to heaven, shall so come in similar manner as you have seen Him go into heaven."

ACTS 1:10–11 SKJV

Jesus had come to earth as a baby and had grown into manhood. He embraced His role as mankind's Redeemer, and His death on the cross confirmed that role. He then rose from the dead, and His disciples watched as He departed again for heaven.

They may have wondered if Jesus would stay with them after His resurrection. He'd been clear that they would need to share His message. And while they must have known He would not be physically present, they were likely confused when He left. Perhaps they were just as grieved as they'd been when they watched Him die.

If they were the sheep, as Jesus had said, then the loss of their shepherd must have been devastating. Hadn't Jesus promised never to abandon them? Wouldn't His Spirit be with them always?

Two figures (likely angels) stood with the men in their confusion and made a stunning promise: Jesus had left them physically. . .but one day, He would return. And in this news, the disciples rediscovered hope—a longing for His return.

Sure, they would miss their friend, but they now knew God was in control. The greatest gift mankind could receive had been delivered. Jesus had experienced what it was like to be one of us, and He left promising to return and take us to where He is. *Mission accomplished.*

HOW SAD AND CONFUSED WOULD YOU HAVE BEEN AS ONE OF JESUS' DISCIPLES WHEN HE LEFT? HOW DOES KNOWING JESUS WILL RETURN PROVIDE COURAGE?

NO MONEY...
BUT SOMETHING BETTER

When [the lame man] saw Peter and John about
to enter, he asked them for some money.
ACTS 3:3 NLT

Peter and John were on the street that day because they were going to attend a prayer service at the temple. It was not uncommon to see people with disabilities lining the streets and begging for financial assistance. The disciples (now known as "apostles") witnessed some of this begging that afternoon.

A man who had been lame since birth was calling to them, begging for money. Many people had no doubt ignored him, and a few had probably imparted some less-than-helpful comments. But Peter and John were different—they stopped to interact. Peter said, "I don't have any silver or gold for you. But I'll give you what I have. In the name of Jesus Christ the Nazarene, get up and walk!" (verse 6 NLT).

For someone who's never walked, how would walking come naturally? Apparently, such questions weren't a problem for this man. He believed. He stood. He walked. Amazingly, the Bible says he even jumped and leaped. People had heard stories of Jesus' healing power, and now His disciples were doing the same thing. But it was always Jesus who made that possible. In fact, it soon became evident that Jesus was still working miracles, despite His absence.

This man, who'd never walked, entered the temple with Peter and John for the prayer service. He undoubtedly had plenty of things to say to God. Verses 9–10 (NLT) says, "All the people saw him walking and heard him praising God. When they realized he was the lame beggar they had seen so often at the Beautiful Gate, they were absolutely astounded!"

HAVE YOU EVER WITNESSED SOMETHING MIRACULOUS
WHEN YOU AGREED TO COOPERATE WITH GOD?
WHY IS IT A GOOD THING THAT GOD CHOOSES TO GIVE YOU
WHAT YOU NEED OVER WHAT YOU MIGHT ASK FOR?

DEFENDING MISBELIEF

*When [the religious leaders] saw the courage of Peter
and John and realized that they were unschooled,
ordinary men, they were astonished and they took
note that these men had been with Jesus.*

ACTS 4:13 NIV

Peter and John had just healed a lame man in the previous
chapter, and now they were in trouble with the less-than-
compassionate religious leaders. These leaders said, "To stop this
thing from spreading any further among the people, we must
warn them to speak no longer to anyone in this name" (verse
17 NIV). They scolded the apostles, threatened them, and had
them spend a night in jail.

But did this fear of God's message tighten the religious
leaders' grip on the people? No—as the lame man stood with
Peter and John, the religious leaders were powerless to stop the
growing impact. The more they tried, the more curious Peter
and John's audience became. Verse 21 (NIV) even says, "They
could not decide how to punish them, because all the people
were praising God for what had happened."

Despite the religious leaders' best efforts to explain or wish it
away, people could see that something amazing was happening.

The power Jesus had brought with Him—and had left with His followers—was enhancing the lives of new believers more than the leaders' teachings ever could.

The leaders found out they simply weren't in control.

Have you ever assumed you knew who Jesus is and what He wants. . .but then found out you were woefully incorrect? Maybe it was because you hadn't spent the time learning from God's Word what is true and what is false. God is the only one who's in control of the truth—so spend time with Him and learn it.

HOW DO YOUR BELIEFS ALTER YOUR ENTIRE WORLDVIEW?
IS GOD ALWAYS YOUR FINAL WORD ON WHAT IS TRUE?

ENCOURAGEMENT GIVEN

Joseph, who was surnamed Barnabas by the apostles
(which is, being interpreted, the son of consolation),
a Levite from the country of Cyprus, having land, sold it
and brought the money and laid it at the apostles' feet.
ACTS 4:36–37 SKJV

His name was Joseph, but you probably know him as Barnabas. He later became a missionary partner of the apostle Paul. Some scholars suggest his brother was one of the seventy who were sent ahead of Jesus to tell others about Him. Or maybe he just had a very personal connection to Jesus and His life-changing message.

When we first hear of Barnabas, he'd just finished selling his land and passing on the entire sum to the apostles. There was always a need among Jesus' followers, so gifts like the one Barnabas brought were much appreciated. Of course, before Barnabas chose to give, he had to have been impressed by God. Giving, after all, always takes trust in God's goodness. It means believing that He knows how to use your gift better than you do.

Perhaps it was Barnabas' trust in God's ability to provide that enabled him to start traveling with the gospel. Whatever the cause, he stayed on the job, no matter how hard things became. He also extended grace to those whose work ethic wasn't quite as strong.

God helped Barnabas stay in control of his thoughts, feelings, and actions. Consequently, he became a vital companion for Paul as they journeyed to tell others about Jesus.

DO YOU HAVE A CLOSE FRIEND WITH WHOM YOU CAN SHARE WHAT YOU'RE LEARNING ABOUT GOD? WHAT DOES THE STORY OF BARNABAS TELL YOU ABOUT ENDURANCE?

THE ADVICE

*"In the present case I advise you: Leave these men alone!
Let them go! For if their purpose or activity is of human origin,
it will fail. But if it is from God, you will not be able to stop
these men; you will only find yourselves fighting against God."*
ACTS 5:38–39 NIV

You've heard of Gamaliel, right? If not, it may surprise you to learn that this man—who was said to be "honored by all the people"—was the unexpected voice of reason in the book of Acts. When his fellow religious leaders amped up their opposition to Jesus, even to the point of jailing those who spoke of Him, Gamaliel asked his fellow Pharisees to relax a bit.

Gamaliel didn't tell the other leaders that they were wrong. He simply suggested that God is always right, no matter what opposing perspectives exist. Here are his exact words: "I advise you: Leave these men alone! Let them go! For if their purpose or activity is of human origin, it will fail. But if it is from God, you will not be able to stop these men; you will only find yourselves fighting against God."

In other words, Gamaliel was suggesting that if they were right and Jesus really were a non-issue, His following would eventually die out for lack of interest. They'd seen this sort of thing before. On the other hand, if this movement really *was* from God, they needed to start asking themselves if they really wanted to resist God or try to stand in His way.

Gamaliel recognized that God was in control—that He didn't need the help of the religious leaders. Therefore, his advice was sound. If people stopped talking about Jesus, God did it. If the teachings of Jesus changed the world. . .God did that too.

HAVE YOU EVER FOUND YOURSELF FIGHTING AGAINST GOD? IF SO, HOW WOULD GAMALIEL'S ADVICE HAVE HELPED YOU?

THE SEVEN

They chose Stephen, a man full of faith and of the Holy Spirit, and Philip, and Prochorus, and Nicanor, and Timon, and Parmenas, and Nicolas, a proselyte of Antioch, whom they set before the apostles.
ACTS 6:5–6 SKJV

You know all about Jesus' twelve disciples, and you've read of the seventy He sent out ahead of Him to preach His good news. Well, Acts 6 introduces *the seven*. You've probably heard of the first two men. (The other five aren't as famous.)

It's possible that earlier, some of these seven men may have been part of the seventy. But at this point, these men weren't preachers, exactly—their job was helping feed the needy. All seven were wise and filled with God's Spirit.

Stephen, for instance, is singled out as a man "full of faith and of the Holy Spirit." Stephen was fearless. He was convinced God was in control. The religious leaders hated him, of course, so they bribed men to publicly lie about Stephen. They said that instead of following God, this man was actively promoting blasphemy.

Stephen defended himself in an eloquent and powerful speech, but just like the crowd who'd called for Jesus' crucifixion, the people couldn't resist rushing toward punishment. So they stoned him. And as the stones found fresh skin, Stephen cried, "Lord Jesus, receive my spirit. . . . Do not lay this sin to their charge" (Acts 7:59–60 SKJV). Then Stephen died.

This story serves as a sobering example of the inhumanity that often arises when prideful people simply won't accept the existence of opposing viewpoints. Neither Jesus nor Stephen tried to get even; instead, they both asked God to forgive their persecutors. This proves that whenever a person gives control to God, kindness and mercy will win within the heart.

IN WHAT WAYS CAN WE STRIVE TO REPRESENT GOD IN ALL ASPECTS OF LIFE? HOW IS SHOWING FORGIVENESS AN IMPORTANT PART OF RECOGNIZING GOD'S CONTROL?

STREET MAGIC

When Simon saw that the Spirit was given when the apostles laid their hands on people, he offered them money to buy this power. "Let me have this power, too," he exclaimed, "so that when I lay my hands on people, they will receive the Holy Spirit!"
ACTS 8:18–19 NLT

Simon (not the fisherman) might seem like someone who owned a carnival. The locals called this man "Simon the Sorcerer"—some even called him "the Great One." Crowds flocked to see his street magic, and Simon loved the attention. So when this first-century street magician saw the apostles performing genuine miracles, he began seeing God as an opportunity to up his game.

Simon liked hanging out with that kind of power. So he learned about Jesus, believed in Jesus, and was baptized. Absent, however, was any notion of repentance. He just wanted to gain the apostles' abilities.

Needless to say, he didn't get what he wanted. So he devised a plan: he'd quietly inquire what it would cost to get the apostles' power. These new tricks would do wonders for his business ventures, giving him added prestige among those who sought a good show.

As you might imagine, this did not sit well with the apostles. They knew God wasn't for sale. For Simon, however, this was a foreign concept. In his mind, *everything* had a price tag. He was used to buying his way into popularity—and to him, the power of God was just another means to that end.

God's power is not for sale (you couldn't afford it anyway), nor is it something He owes you. It's a gift. It's not a business transaction—it's a life transformation.

HAVE YOU EVER FELT THAT GOD OWES YOU SOMETHING
HE NEVER PROMISED? WHY IS IT IMPORTANT
TO REALIZE GOD'S POWER IS A GIFT?

CHANGE OF HEART

As [Saul] neared Damascus on his journey, suddenly a light from heaven flashed around him. He fell to the ground and heard a voice say to him, "Saul, Saul, why do you persecute me?"
ACTS 9:3–4 NIV

Saul had permission to punish anyone who followed Jesus. And the religious leaders (who wanted this movement to end) gave him the green light to persecute. They provided him with letters to the synagogue in Damascus voicing their support. If Saul found Christians there, he was encouraged to take them as prisoners to Jerusalem. He was prepared to do whatever it took to stop people from following Jesus.

Suddenly, however, he was temporarily struck blind. In this new place of darkness, Saul met Jesus. "Why do you persecute me?" was the question this risen Savior had for Saul.

God's Word never says that Saul answered this question. He did, however, have time to think about it. Saul's friends led him into the city, where he spent three days in darkness—neither eating nor drinking. Saul probably spent a lot of that time rethinking his life choices.

This persecutor of Christians did have a change of heart, mind, and name. Shortly thereafter, Jesus said of him, "This man is my chosen instrument to proclaim my name to the Gentiles and their kings and to the people of Israel" (verse 15 NIV).

Saul, whom we know better as Paul, eventually became an apostle to all people outside of Israel. For years, Christian Jews were understandably suspicious of him: after all, what if he was just faking his missionary work? But God was in complete control, and He used Paul not only to save Christians' lives but to show the world that Jesus is the ultimate difference maker.

Never assume that God can't turn even the worst offender into a sold-out follower of Christ.

DO YOU EVER ASSUME SOME PEOPLE WILL NEVER SEE
A NEED FOR JESUS? IF SO, HOW CAN SAUL'S STORY
MOTIVATE YOU TO PRAY FOR THESE PEOPLE?

THE RELIEF FUND

In these days prophets came from Jerusalem to Antioch.
And one of them named Agabus stood up and signified by the
Spirit that there would be great famine throughout all the world.
ACTS 11:27–28 SKJV

Agabus the prophet is only mentioned twice—both times in the book of Acts. Similar to Joseph's prediction to Pharaoh, Agabus had some bad news: a famine was coming.

The predictions of true prophets always come true. . .and Agabus was a true prophet. But why does Acts 11 mention this prophecy? Maybe because in retrospect, this bad news led to something beautiful. The famine came, but the people wouldn't prepare by storing grain like Joseph had. No, preparation would come through first-century crowdfunding. (God calls it an offering.) Countless Christians banded together to send a financial gift to those who would be affected by the famine.

Not only did God provide for those who would need the help, but He did it in a way that likely surprised those who still had concerns about Paul: He used Paul as part of the delivery service. Some might have wondered if the money would actually reach its destination. They no doubt wondered about Paul, but they trusted God even more. And because of that trust—and because of Agabus' obedience in sharing his "bad news"—the famine relief fund was finally gathered. What's more, Paul's ministry would soon be instrumental in introducing Jesus to the desperate and hopeless.

This is just another step on the ladder that leads to the observation deck of all the ways God is in control. Not even bad news and persecution can thwart His design.

WHAT DOES THIS STORY TEACH US ABOUT TRUST?
WHEN BAD NEWS IS RAINING DOWN, DO YOU KEEP
BELIEVING GOD IS MAINTAINING CONTROL?

UNEXPECTED DELIVERANCE

When Herod saw how much this pleased the
Jewish people, he also arrested Peter.
ACTS 12:3 NLT

Perhaps feeling the need to appease the Christ-hating religious leaders, King Herod Agrippa began persecuting those who insisted on talking about Jesus. Herod even had the apostle James executed. And after the Jewish people cheered that decision, he arrested Peter, planning to do the same to him. . .and to anyone else who refused to be quiet about Jesus.

This could have caused Jesus' followers to fall silent, run away, and deny Him. But it didn't. Instead, verse 5 (NLT) says, "While Peter was in prison, the church prayed very earnestly for him."

As the sun set on the night before Peter's highly public trial, God was secretly answering prayers. Peter was chained up and guarded by soldiers, but in the middle of the night, the chains fell off. Then God's messenger angel told Peter to walk out of prison.

Soon, Peter arrived at the house where Jesus' followers were praying for him. When he knocked on the door, a servant named Rhoda answered. She was so startled that she left him outside and ran to tell the others. Eventually, Peter was allowed to come inside and share his unbelievable story.

The next morning, King Herod sent soldiers to look for Peter. They couldn't find him, however, and Herod packed up his belongings and went to stay in Caesarea. Consequently, "the word of God continued to spread, and there were many new believers" (verse 24 NLT). God's message didn't stop because of a vengeful king, as seen by the fact that it has reached you today.

Bad things will happen—trouble is a constant for anyone who breathes. God never promised a life free of struggle, but He has provided an all-access pass to talk with Him.

He's already overcome our trouble. . .and His victory is irreversible.

WHY DO YOU THINK TROUBLE IS AN INESCAPABLE PART OF LIFE? HOW HAVE YOU SEEN GOD CONTROL TROUBLE?

BECOMING USEFUL

They had such a sharp disagreement that they parted company. Barnabas took Mark and sailed for Cyprus.
Acts 15:39 niv

Paul and Barnabas were missionary partners—it's hard to think of one without thinking of the other. They believed in the same God, shared the story of Jesus, and cared deeply for people. But the Bible mentions one disagreement that was sharp enough to temporarily send the two men going in different directions.

Here's the backstory. John Mark was a young missionary who went on a trip with Paul, and then he just went home. We don't know if he even told anyone why. He just. . .left. Some scholars say he did more than leave—that he may have also given a bad report about Paul. This young man seemed unreliable at best, a troublemaker at worst.

Barnabas, clearly seeking to give John Mark a second chance, wanted to bring him along on another journey. Paul, however, seemed certain this was a bad idea. The argument grew so heated that Paul chose a new ministry partner (Silas) and headed toward Syria while Barnabas took Mark and headed to Cyprus. Both sets of ministry partners had the same agenda—to make

Christ known—but they weren't in the right place to pursue that agenda together.

In time, the rift was mended, as seen by Paul's words in 2 Timothy 4:11 (NIV): "Get Mark and bring him with you, because he is helpful to me in my ministry."

Barnabas learned patience, Paul learned grace, and John Mark learned God's power to restore fractured relationships. And as a side note, it's believed that God used John Mark to write the Gospel of Mark. God never fails to find a place for anyone who wants to be useful.

DO YOU TEND TO GIVE UP ON PEOPLE WHO LET YOU DOWN? HOW CAN WE APPLY GRACE WHILE WORKING WITH OTHER CHRISTIANS?

THE APPRENTICE

*Then he came to Derbe and Lystra. And behold, a certain
disciple was there named Timothy, the son of a certain
Jewish woman who believed, but his father was a Greek.*

ACTS 16:1 SKJV

While continuing his missionary journey with Silas, Paul met
a young man named Timothy. In that place and time, this
young man was likely seen as a misfit. Timothy's mother was a
Jew who followed Jesus, and his father was a Greek. As a result,
many Jews didn't see him as a Jew, and many Greeks didn't see
him as a Greek. Yet Paul saw something in this young man.

The apostle invested time with this apprentice. He taught
him, encouraged him, and gave him responsibility. Eventually,
Paul would write two letters to Timothy. In one letter, he spoke
these words of encouragement: "Do not let any man despise
your youth, but be an example to the believers in word, in
conversation, in love, in spirit, in faith, in purity. Until I come,
give attendance to reading, to exhortation, to doctrine. Do not
neglect the gift that is in you" (1 Timothy 4:12–14 SKJV).

Paul even referred to Timothy as a true son in the faith.
Clearly, something had happened in Paul after refusing to work
with John Mark. The process of working with Timothy seemed

to have softened the man who had once persecuted Christians. Maybe this was due to his gradual realization that God, not Paul, was in control.

Who you are today is not what you have to be tomorrow. Allow God to start smoothing the rough edges, learn from Him, and accept that you are His true son in the faith. Let Him make you new.

HOW HAS GOD SOFTENED YOU SINCE YOU ACCEPTED HIS RESCUE PLAN? HOW DOES THIS SOFTENING CHANGE THE WAY YOU SEE OTHERS?

THE EXPANSION

*A Jew named Apollos, an eloquent speaker. . .had been
taught the way of the Lord, and he taught others about
Jesus with an enthusiastic spirit and with accuracy.*
ACTS 18:24–25 NLT

Apollos lived in Ephesus, where he was winning friends and
influencing people by teaching about Jesus. He was both enthusiastic and eloquent, so whenever he spoke, people paid attention and remembered what he said. But he also loved to learn.
Therefore, whenever God sent people who knew more about
Jesus, Apollos listened and added this new information into
his message.

These people encouraged Apollos to tell those in Achaia
what he knew about Jesus. Next, "they wrote to the believers in
Achaia, asking them to welcome him. When he arrived there,
he proved to be of great benefit to those who, by God's grace,
had believed" (verse 27 NLT).

Apollos hadn't been a disciple, apostle, or even one of the
seven or seventy. But the depth of Jesus' teaching was informing
a new generation of Christian leaders. Given that all humans
die, this good news would need to be passed on to future generations. . .so that they, too, could pass it on.

The Bible isn't just a collection of unrelated, irrelevant stories about how the ancients responded to God's call. Rather, it consistently illustrates God's control by describing how His message trickled down to each successive generation. God didn't want to wall off His message; He wanted its popularity to expand until it reached everyone.

After Jesus' Great Commission (see Matthew 28:18–20), this new movement started small. But it grew and continues to grow. Eventually, it would find its home in the hearts of countless believers who helped change the world. . .leading all the way up to you.

DOES THE STORY OF APOLLOS INSPIRE YOU TO FOLLOW GOD'S LEADING? HOW MIGHT YOU TELL OTHERS ABOUT GOD TODAY?

A SHIFT IN COMMERCE

There arose a great disturbance about the Way. A silversmith named Demetrius, who made silver shrines of Artemis, brought in a lot of business for the craftsmen there.
ACTS 19:23–24 NIV

None of us are strangers to opposition—we inevitably face it whenever we find the courage to voice our opinions and convictions. Paul, however, seemed to be more familiar with opposition than most.

As Paul was preaching about the Way (an early name for Christianity), many people were listening and making changes. Even commerce was being affected by this fledgling movement. Demetrius, for instance, was a businessman whose occupation was on the verge of collapse because of Paul. Why? Because his primary moneymakers were objects related to the false god Artemis. He apparently was connected to many skilled artisans who kept up with public demand for their metal objects, but demand was rapidly declining. As a result, he became an outspoken advocate for shutting Paul down.

In a speech that must have seemed practical and eloquent to his audience, he said,

"You see and hear how this fellow Paul has convinced and led astray large numbers of people here in Ephesus and in practically the whole province of Asia. He says that gods made by human hands are no gods at all. There is danger not only that our trade will lose its good name, but also that the temple of the great goddess Artemis will be discredited; and the goddess herself, who is worshiped throughout the province of Asia and the world, will be robbed of her divine majesty."
ACTS 19:26–27 NIV

But whenever opposition is the fiercest, that's when God—who's always in control—makes Himself known. Persecution is often a setup for the sweeping introduction of God's grace, love, and forgiveness in the hearts of those who've spent their lives worshipping the wrong thing.

WHY DOES GIVING UP SEEM SO EASY WHENEVER SOMEONE OPPOSES GOD'S MESSAGE? HAVE YOU EVER WITNESSED OPPOSITION TO GOD TRANSFORM INTO ACCEPTANCE?

DEEP SLEEP

*A certain young man named Eutychus sat in a window,
having fallen into a deep sleep. And as Paul was long
preaching, he sunk down with sleep and fell down
from the third loft and was taken up dead.*

ACTS 20:9 SKJV

Eutychus probably didn't set out to fall asleep during a sermon
by the apostle Paul. Then again, it's likely no one thought Paul
would preach all night. So as Eutychus sat by a window in the
third loft, listening attentively and learning, things started growing fuzzy. His eyes gradually closed, and Paul's voice faded into
an imperceptible drone. Eutychus' young body grew limp. . .then
sleep overtook him.

That's when something unexpected and tragic happened:
Eutychus fell out of the window where he'd been sitting. He
died on impact.

Of course, Paul's sermon came to a halt as everyone noticed
what had happened. The apostle went outside, threw his arms
around the dead man, and proclaimed that Eutychus was alive.
Suddenly, life returned to the young man. The Bible doesn't
give Eutychus' response, so we don't know if he was embarrassed, confused, or apologetic. All we know was that he started

breathing again. As this young man continued in his journey with God, he probably thought often of this day.

At times we're all embarrassed by things in our lives, and we seek to explain our actions. Well, Eutychus had been *dead*, and now he was walking around—just try to explain that! For His part, God cared more about Eutychus than He did about explaining Himself. This young man was a living example of God's grace—and that's the only explanation we need.

HAVE YOU EVER "FALLEN ASLEEP" SPIRITUALLY,
ONLY TO WAKE UP REALIZING YOU NEEDED GOD'S HELP?
HOW CAN YOUR MISSTEPS PROVE GOD IS IN CONTROL?

ASSASSINATION PLOT

*Paul's nephew—his sister's son—heard of their
plan and went to the fortress and told Paul.*

ACTS 23:16 NLT

- -

Acts 23 describes an assassination plot in which forty men waited
to put an end to the apostle Paul's life. This plot included even
the leading religious rulers of the day, and they vowed not to
eat or drink anything until Paul was dead.

Paul, however, had a young nephew (we don't know his
name) who didn't want to see his uncle hurt. So this young man
devised a plan: he would reveal the plot, ask for an audience with
the commander in charge of protecting Paul, and make him
aware of the dangers of transporting Paul to the high council.

The plan worked. Soon, Paul found himself traveling by
night to Governor Felix in Caesarea, surrounded by more than
250 soldiers. Having heard there was no fault found in Paul,
but wanting to hear the charges for himself, the governor placed
the apostle in prison to await his accusers.

This probably wasn't the outcome Paul's nephew had hoped
for. Perhaps he blamed himself for what happened to his uncle.
Maybe he rehashed in his mind what more he could have
done. In the end, however, God used this seemingly unfair

imprisonment to give Paul the opportunity to share the gospel to the high rulers. Now his words would be heard by more people than ever before. And even in prison, God took care of Paul and gave him fresh grace.

When plans backfire and nothing seems to go the way you want, remember that God may be setting you up for a unique chance to make an impact in someone's life.

DOES A CHRISTIAN EVER HAVE A REASON TO WORRY?
WHY OR WHY NOT? HAS GOD EVER TAKEN A CONFUSING MESS
IN YOUR LIFE AND TURNED IT INTO A REASON FOR WORSHIP?

THE SHIPWRECK

When it was decided that we would sail for Italy,
Paul and some other prisoners were handed over to a centurion
named Julius, who belonged to the Imperial Regiment.

ACTS 27:1 NIV

What began as a rescue mission had led to Paul's spending more than two years in prison. It seems the various rulers couldn't decide what to do with him. But now that Paul had appealed to Caesar, his seafaring journey to Rome was about to begin.

Julius the centurion (a man who commanded a hundred soldiers) was in charge of transferring Paul and other prisoners to Italy. But despite his vigilance, the less-than-ideal conditions surrounding the journey might have put Julius ill at ease. Nevertheless, he showed kindness to Paul by allowing him to spend time with friends in Sidon at one of the stops along the way. Once they departed Sidon, things were about to get much worse.

After days of little headway, Paul said, "Men, I can see that our voyage is going to be disastrous and bring great loss to ship and cargo, and to our own lives also" (verse 10 NIV). The ship had encountered a northeaster—a powerful wind that pushed them back the way they came and forced them to strap ropes around the ship to keep it together. For days, the sun did not shine.

That's when one of God's angels came to the apostle Paul with this message: "Do not be afraid, Paul. You must stand trial before Caesar; and God has graciously given you the lives of all who sail with you" (verse 24 NIV). Paul insisted that everyone eat, and then they waited for the inevitable shipwreck. The "proper" procedure was to kill the prisoners to prevent them from escaping, but Julius commanded his soldiers not to harm anyone.

This shipwreck could have been a complete disaster. But God's intervention ensured a memorable, miraculous conclusion.

HOW CAN GOD'S ORCHESTRATION OF EVENTS CAUSE EVEN OUR ENEMIES TO BECOME HELPFUL? HOW DOES PAUL'S SHIPWRECK STORY CHALLENGE YOU TO TRUST GOD MORE?

THE DETOUR

In the same region were lands of the chief man of the island, whose name was Publius, who received us and lodged us courteously three days.

ACTS 28:7 SKJV

This is the conclusion to yesterday's shipwreck story.

The nearly three hundred passengers of the doomed ship eventually washed up on the shore of an island called Malta. There, the residents offered them warmth and shelter. How likely would most people be to offer help to such a ragged lot of prisoners and soldiers? Many would probably keep their distance, and no one would blame them. Thankfully, the residents of Malta were more compassionate than most.

As the ship's occupants warmed themselves by a fire, the apostle Paul stepped in to help by gathering wood. Suddenly, a viper sprang out of the brush and latched on to his hand. The people immediately assumed Paul must have somehow displeased their gods. But when Paul shook off the snake and continued his wood gathering as if nothing had happened, they immediately thought, *Maybe he* is *one of our gods!* Paul, of course, rejected their worship, using it instead as an opportunity to teach about Jesus.

The leader of the island was a man named Publius. He seemed taken with Paul and invited him and others to stay at his house. Publius' father was very sick with a high fever, so Paul prayed for this man. . .and he was healed. Word spread like wildfire—soon, every sick person in Malta was rushing to see Paul, and they were all healed as well.

Paul's wintertime trip to Rome would stick with him for the rest of his life, but so would Publius, Julius, Paul's nearly three hundred fellow passengers, and this entire island who witnessed God's work firsthand. It seems this shipwreck was simply a detour that God used to further spread His goodness.

WHEN IT SEEMS YOU'VE BEEN SET ASIDE,
HOW CAN YOU LOOK FOR WAYS TO BE USED BY GOD?
HAS AN UNEXPECTED LIFE DETOUR EVER BROUGHT
YOU FACE-TO-FACE WITH GOD'S PLAN?

A FRIEND'S GREETING

Greet Andronicus and Junia, my fellow Jews, who were in prison with me. They are highly respected among the apostles and became followers of Christ before I did.
ROMANS 16:7 NLT

Paul wasn't in prison for just a couple days or even a couple weeks. He stayed in jail for at least two years. Imagine how discouraged he must have felt. . .had God not been actively supplying encouragement in the form of His own presence and two fellow prisoners.

Andronicus and Junia were both Jews, just like Paul, and they both followed Jesus. Some scholars believe they may have been husband and wife, and they may have also been a part of the seventy that Jesus had sent out earlier.

Regardless of why they were in prison, their life experiences were likely similar to Paul's. They were probably witnesses to Jesus' work—whether they saw Him in person or saw His world-shaking power working through a new generation of believers.

While these two may be all but lost to history, the importance of the encouragement they offered Paul in prison cannot be overstated. They were so significant to him that he greeted them as close friends at the end of the book of Romans.

The friends you make (and those you keep) often directly impact the way you deal with life's challenges. They can influence your choice to either stand strong or head to the sidelines. God wants you to have friends and be a friend, but He also wants you to choose wisely.

So today, ask God to help you recognize good friends. They may not always be obvious, but God will bring them along when they're needed most.

HOW MIGHT PAUL'S GREETING CHANGE THE WAY YOU SEE YOUR OWN FRIENDSHIPS? HAVE GOOD FRIENDS MADE A POSITIVE IMPACT IN YOUR LIFE LIKE THEY DID IN PAUL'S?

THE BODY

There are different kinds of gifts, but the same
Spirit distributes them. There are different
kinds of service, but the same Lord. There are
different kinds of working, but in all of them
and in everyone it is the same God at work.

1 CORINTHIANS 12:4–6 NIV

Good stories usually include the names of primary characters. This, however, is a good story without names. It's an illustration Paul used while writing to the church family in Corinth. His readers seemed to be confused, and Paul knew the power of stories when it comes to clearing things up.

This story is all about how the body functions. It's not a biology lesson; rather, it's an object lesson. Imagine a human body that's nothing but a hand (or an eye or an ear). It would be useless outside of its one component's very specific function. A hand, for instance, can hold things. . .but it can't see. An eye can see, but it can't walk. An ear can hear but can't talk.

This seems obvious to us humans, but it was God's idea to assemble the complex structure of the human body and make it work. And He does exactly the same for the body of Christ. The problem arises when certain members start believing they're more important than the others. When that happens, vital members of the church are ignored and the body as a whole begins crumbling from within.

The church at Corinth would have recognized themselves in this story. They were being driven by selfishness. . .and selfishness is poison to the body of Christ.

This lesson was for the church at Corinth, but it's also been for everyone throughout history. You may not have the same gifts as other Christians, but God wants you to use your gifts so that He can use your willingness.

WHAT ROLES WITHIN THE CHURCH DO YOU THINK ARE MOST IMPORTANT? WHY? HOW IS GOD'S CONTROL MADE EVIDENT WHENEVER THE BODY OF CHRIST WORKS TOGETHER?

THE GIFT

Now concerning the collection for the saints, as I have given order to the churches of Galatia, even you do also. On the first day of the week, let each one of you lay aside something to store, as God has prospered you, that there are no collections when I come. And when I come, whomever you shall approve, I will send them with your letters to bring your gift to Jerusalem.

1 CORINTHIANS 16:1–3 SKJV

It seemed some people in the church at Corinth had the wrong ideas about giving to God. Either they thought giving implied God wasn't big enough to take care of things on His own, or they thought it was pointless because God didn't need their money, so they might as well keep it.

They weren't the only ones to struggle with this—Paul indicated he had given the church in Galatia similar instruction. God could use giving to bring help to others. After all, God created all the raw components we use, as well as the ability to earn an income, so He's certainly in control of what happens when we give.

Giving back to God is a way to worship the one who has never failed to meet your needs. It teaches you about compassion, empathy, and kindness. Consequently, giving must be intentional and timely.

You don't give simply because God asks you to; you give to show that you care about others. Your gift shows that God has been doing something in your life that reaches far beyond your own wants and needs. Giving shows that other people are important to you. . .and that God is the most important of them all.

HOW WOULD YOU FEEL IF YOU WERE IN THE CORINTHIANS' SHOES, RECEIVING CORRECTION FROM PAUL ON THE TOPIC OF GIVING? WOULD YOU BE UNCOMFORTABLE? GRATEFUL? WHY?

MAGNIFIED AND HIDEOUS

[Paul said,] "I am not sorry that I sent that severe letter to you, though I was sorry at first, for I know it was painful to you for a little while."

2 Corinthians 7:8 NLT

Lots of people dislike their employee evaluations. They can seem unfair, unhelpful, and intrusive. Workers may feel they lower their morale and cause anxiety.

This was likely how the members of the church at Corinth felt. Paul had written a letter to them that pointed out their flaws. Consequently, they may have felt like they couldn't do anything right. And as they talked the situation over among themselves, some may have even said some hurtful things about Paul.

In this second letter to the Christians in Corinth, Paul suggests it was hard to write the letter. He knew it could be taken very badly. The magnifying glass of scrutiny, after all, is rarely welcome. It exposes ugly character flaws and actions. It draws attention to selfishness. So it's safe to say the Corinthian church hadn't enjoyed it either.

Paul, however, put the pain in perspective:

Now I am glad I sent it, not because it hurt you, but

because the pain caused you to repent and change your ways. It was the kind of sorrow God wants his people to have, so you were not harmed by us in any way. For the kind of sorrow God wants us to experience leads us away from sin and results in salvation. There's no regret for that kind of sorrow.

2 CORINTHIANS 7:9–10 NLT

God is in control, so He already knows when our hearts are deceptive. He doesn't expose this deceit to make us angry; rather, He does it to induce a sorrow that leads us back to Him.

WHEN'S THE LAST TIME THAT HEARING THE TRUTH MADE YOU ANGRY? HOW LONG DID IT TAKE FOR THAT ANGER TO TURN TO SORROW AS YOU ALLOWED GOD TO REDIRECT YOUR STEPS?

KNOCK IT OFF

*As I urged you when I went into Macedonia,
stay there in Ephesus so that you may command certain
people not to teach false doctrines any longer.*
1 Timothy 1:3 niv

The apostle Paul left Timothy, whom he considered his son in the faith, in Ephesus to oversee the church there. Timothy was young, but he was also a steadfast follower of Jesus. Paul trusted him.

One of the things Paul noticed was that some people were speaking falsehoods about God's words and actions. Paul said, "Some have departed from these and have turned to meaningless talk. They want to be teachers of the law, but they do not know what they are talking about" (verses 6–7 niv). When people believed this false teaching, they began reinterpreting what God had actually said and done, trying to make it fit their mistaken beliefs.

Paul said that one of Timothy's primary jobs was to clearly tell these false teachers to stop. He didn't suggest that they tame it down or take a remedial course in religious studies. Timothy was to command them to *stop*. They were simply causing too much damage for Timothy to turn a blind eye.

These people wanted to be seen as authorities on their own made-up beliefs. But as with everything else, truth is controlled by God, not humans. God wanted to make His thoughts completely clear for future generations, so He had them written down. And whenever we choose to accept something extra or remove things we don't like, we end up believing something contrary to God's truth.

God wants you to see life—even when it gets ugly—through the lens of His truth.

IN WHAT WAYS DOES CULTURE TRY CONVINCING US THAT GOD NO LONGER MEANS WHAT HE SAID IN THE BIBLE? IF GOD WERE TO CHANGE HIS MIND, WHAT WOULD THAT SAY ABOUT THE EXTENT OF HIS CONTROL?

LEADERSHIP IDENTIFICATION

I left you on the island of Crete so you could complete our work there and appoint elders in each town as I instructed you. An elder must live a blameless life. He must be faithful to his wife, and his children must be believers who don't have a reputation for being wild or rebellious.

TITUS 1:5–6 NLT

Titus was another younger man whom Paul mentored. The apostle had left him on the island of Crete, and like Timothy, he had a very important job: he was in charge of identifying the leadership teams for the churches on Crete.

Paul had once preached at Crete, and now that people were accepting God's salvation, the question of leadership roles naturally arose. And as Paul listed qualifications for the ideal leader, he said, "He must have a strong belief in the trustworthy message he was taught; then he will be able to encourage others with wholesome teaching and show those who oppose it where they are wrong" (verse 9 NLT).

Titus' job differed from Timothy's, Timothy's differed from Apollos', and Apollos' differed from Paul's. Yet each of these men recognized their gift and used it for a singular purpose—to expand the reach of the soul-saving message of Jesus' life, death, and resurrection.

You can find your place by living this way. Instead of wanting to imitate someone else or strike out alone, you can simply look for where God is working. . .and offer to help in whatever way you can. It will probably be awkward at first. You won't be "the best" at your job. But you'll be where God wants you, and that's all that matters.

Ordinary men do extraordinary things whenever they're willing to trust and obey God's plan for their lives.

ARE YOU SEEKING TO APPLY YOUR SPIRITUAL SKILL
SET TOWARD DOING GOD'S WORK? IN WHAT WAYS
HAS GOD REVEALED THESE TALENTS TO YOU?

HOME AGAIN

Although in Christ I could be bold and order you to do what you ought to do, yet I prefer to appeal to you on the basis of love.
PHILEMON 1:8–9 NIV

Even in prison, Paul had great authority in the church, having mentored many people who were now becoming great leaders. While in chains, Paul met a man named Onesimus. It's not clear if this younger man was simply a visitor or if he, too, was in prison.

Every man has a past. . .and not all want to share it. But in time, Onesimus grew to trust Paul enough to tell him his story. It seems this man had been a servant of one of Paul's friends, Philemon. But Onesimus ran away, abandoning his post with no intention to return.

Was it possible that a much older Paul was remembering his disagreement with Barnabas over another young man who had run away—John Mark? Could he have been thinking about his mentorship of Timothy and Titus and how his encouragement had unlocked their full potential?

We'll never know. But we do know that Paul now saw himself as a mediator between two men: a deserter and his former master, who may have still harbored bitterness. Consequently, this is one of Paul's gentlest letters—an invitation for a friend to forgive a friend. Paul said, "If you consider me a partner, welcome him as you would welcome me. If he has done you any wrong or owes you anything, charge it to me" (verses 17–18 NIV).

God is in control because He sent His Son, Jesus, as the mediator between Himself and us. And He is inviting every one of us to return home as forgiven, restored sons in the faith.

WHY DOES GOD VALUE RESTORING BROKEN RELATIONSHIPS
SO MUCH? HOW DOES HIS ABILITY TO RESTORE
PROVE THAT HE'S ALWAYS IN CONTROL?

THE TRUSTED KING JAMES VERSION. . . JUST EASIER TO READ

God Is in Control Devotions for Men quotes scripture from the Barbour Simplified KJV. Maintaining the familiarity and trustworthiness of the King James Version, it removes the difficulties of antiquated language and punctuation. Keeping all the original translation work of the 1611 Bible, the Simplified KJV carefully updates old styles that may interfere with your reading pleasure and comprehension today.

Read it for FREE! Download at
www.SimplifiedKJV.com